By the same author:
The Distasteful Challenge (1968)
The Decade of Upheaval: Irish Trade Unions in the Nineteen Sixties (1973)
Trade Unions in Ireland 1894 to 1960 (1977)

Charles McCarthy

ELEMENTS IN A THEORY OF INDUSTRIAL RELATIONS

IRISH ACADEMIC PRESS

This book was typeset by Printset & Design Ltd.,
Dublin, and was printed in Ireland for
Irish Academic Press Ltd., Kill Lane, Blackrock,
Co. Dublin.

ISBN 0-7165-2363-9

Preface

It is clear that I was greatly stimulated, in attempting this study, by the work of H.L.A. Hart. Nonetheless there is a sense in which, in industrial relations, one is in a more primitive condition in regard to the law than that which exists in society generally and which Professor Hart discusses. If one can on the whole assume some consensual basis for law in society, although its philosophical basis may be shrouded in difficulty, one can assume no such consensus in regard to what is legitimate in industrial relations. Here indeed the law is evolving, not in the sense merely of the description of the concept, but in the very way in which the parties to the process are struggling to find a common understanding of what is right, so that some reasonable body of rules can be created. This book is an attempt to explore the issues, to mark the areas in which consensus is readily enough achieved and to mark as well the areas where the chasm is great.

The major reason for the study springs from the present debate on the role of law in industrial relations, a debate that has taken on some of the character of trench warfare and seems just as fruitless. My hope is that this analysis may recast the questions in a way that will invite some answers and some initiatives that have not arisen before.

Two points of method in the book may be of help. The first is to use the logic of jurisprudence rather than to use the logic of administrative effectiveness, to ask, not how one gives the Labour Court, for example, more status administratively but rather to ask what the nature of its legitimacy is, and on what general rule of law, understood in its widest sense, does this legitimacy rest.

The second point of method (and in this I depart from the traditional approach of the jurist) is to insist on seeing all these matters from the point of view of the parties, seeking their best interest, impatient of constraint, and bound by the obligation they owe to others only in so far as it appears to them to be legitimate that they should be. This permits me to explore the contrast between freedoms and rights in a manner which is largely imperceptible to the traditional juridical approach, which sees things primarily from the poit of view of the court, of the adjudicator, of the person engaged in the application of the law rather than of the person who is painfully identifying it in the course of his own activity.

I am grateful to Mr Michael Doherty of the Computer Laboratory, Trinity College, for his generosity in providing essential technical advice in the production of this book, to the Irish Management Institute for this welcome subvention to its cost, to Mr Michael Adams of the Irish Academic Press for his imaginative support, but above all to Ms Ruth McLoughlin of the School of Business and Administrative Studies of Trinity College who by her skill and considerable technical insight made the present production possible.

To the memory of
FRANCIS STEWART LELAND LYONS
Provost of Trinity College 1974-1981

CONTENTS

CHAPTER ONE

The Placing of the Subject

1

This is an attempt at some theoretical understanding of what we call industrial relations. Our concern is with relations in the workplace, with relations between organised labour and employers deriving from the workplace, and in particular with the circumstances in which such relations fall into dispute.

Industrial relations as a subject of academic inquiry has become more and more popular in recent years; but it is an odd area. Unlike sociology or physics it is clearly not itself a method, a discipline, an organised way of looking at the world, but rather the subject matter of such a method. Now if one wishes to rise above an elementary descriptive account of the institutions and their activities, one has to embrace some academic convention. Whether one embraces it critically or not is beside the point; the discipline itself is in all probability essential as an approach. It brings to the study an opportunity for the generalising of knowledge, for the building of scholarship one step upon another and an opportunity for mutual evaluation. It is difficult to see how the organised scholarship of the universities would be possible without it.

And yet there is a danger — which of course is well recognised. It rests in the very coherence of the community of learning and also its dominance. A particular community is determined by the body of theoretical knowledge which is accepted as a foundation, and which, although it may in part be denied, remains the point of reference and understanding; from it spring the criteria by which scholarship and research are judged. Furthermore, its dominance is such that a social scientist for example has been described as one who is 'socialised' into the scientific community. He must accept the rules which determine what counts as an experiment and what is an explanatory hypothesis. Learning the current 'paradigm' is learning the rules of scientific life.[1]

It is true, of course, that the social sciences unlike the natural sciences appear to speak with numerous tongues, causing more than one writer to urge the wisdom of a single terminology which would govern mathematical sociologists and behaviourists, structuralists, marxists and phenomenologists (although the better view appears to be that such a venture is not only impossible but wrongheaded).[2] But the existence of such a babel does not lessen the imperiousness of the various schools, inevitable perhaps if they are to retain their sense of rigour. And that is where the danger lies, because an inquiry is undertaken as a rule by a person heavily committed to a very specialised way of looking at the world which has its own coherence and rationality, and this may result in the imposition on the area to be studied of such formalism with regard to assumptions, such formalism with regard to meaning and relevance, as to distort, sometimes substantially, the very object for which the exercise has been designed.

When therefore we come to consider industrial relations and how it might be approached, it is necessary to review these various disciplines, even if only in a brief and superficial way, in order to justify the appropriateness of the approach which is suggested here. In the United Kingdom, in Ireland and in the United States, industrial relations as an area has been cultivated principally by the social scientist, that is to say, in very general terms, the sociologist and the economist, the psychologist and the anthropologist. We do not suggest that method here, and it is therefore necessary to ask at the outset of our endeavour, why and in what sense the notion of social science is not the preferred approach.

2

In order to assess appropriateness, it is necessary to identify the central preoccupation of those who are engaged in industrial relations and who are profoundly influenced by it. Again and again one is struck by the concern with right and wrong, with notions of rule and its observance, with procedures and proprieties related to correct behaviour, however much they might be departed from at one time or another. In a word, it appears that the central preoccupation consists in the idea of obligation, the implications of obligation and the means by which it can be vindicated. It finds its characteristic expression as an idea in positive law, but, with industrial relations in particular, it is inevitably larger than that, covering not only notions of fundamental right but at the other extreme conventions and practices which are often ill-defined and sometimes very transient. We shall develop this idea more fully later, but, if for the purpose of this discussion we accept the notion of obligation as a necessary element of our investigation, then, it is suggested, the approach of the social sciences in general appears to be inadequate. For a compelling view along these lines, let us look to H.L.A.Hart, who, while not identifying for criticism the social sciences as such, nevertheless provides probably one of the most serious evaluations of their inadequacy in a situation which is concerned with obligation and its expression in rule. Hart was writing of the broad concept of law not with its particular expression in industrial relations, but his exploration of obligation has considerable force. In a passage which is concerned with its analysis[3] he is troubled by the limitations of what he describes as the predictive theory, which defines obligation 'in terms of the likelihood that threatened punishment or hostile reaction will follow deviation from certain lines of conduct.'[4] That such a fear can exist is no doubt true, but the characteristic of obligation lies not in that but in the idea of rule which is socially significant, under which the case of the person experiencing the obligation has fallen. Until the importance of this point is grasped, writes Professor Hart, 'we cannot properly understand the whole distinctive style of human thought, speech and action which is involved in the existence of rules and which constitutes the normative structure of society.'[5]

But what in fact do we mean by predictive theory? Hart in his elucidation developed it by distinguishing between the external and the internal aspects of rule, because in the case of rules of conduct one may be concerned with them either merely as an observer who does not himself accept them, or as a member of the group which accepts them and uses them as guides to conduct.

These Hart calls respectively the external and internal points of view. In a well-known passage, which bears repetition here, he uses, to describe the external point of view, the image of an observer at a traffic junction:

His view will be like the view of one, who, having observed the working of a traffic signal in a busy street for some time, limits himself to saying that when the light turns red there is a high probability that the traffic will stop. He treats the light merely as a natural *sign that* people will behave in certain ways, as clouds are a *sign that* rain will come. In so doing he will miss out a whole dimension of the social life of those whom he is watching, since for them the red light is not merely a sign that others will stop; they look upon it as a *signal for* them to stop, and so a reason for stopping in conformity to rules which make stopping when the light is red a standard of behaviour and an obligation. To mention this is to bring into account the way in which the group regards its own behaviour. It is to refer to the internal aspect of rules seen from their internal point of view.[6]

While a person relying merely on this predictive view might well behave in society in a manner indistinguishable from a person who recognised rule as a guide of conduct, he could, if asked to explain his actions, say only that he was obliged to take a certain course, conveying thereby that he would suffer if he deviated from it. He would be unable to say 'I had an obligation' for such a phrase has meaning only for those who see their cwn and others' conduct from an internal point of view. And yet such a notion as recognising obligation is a necessary basis for claims, demands, admissions, criticism or punishment, that is to say 'in all the familiar transactions of life according to rules.'[7]

Let us deal with a difficulty at this point in the manner in which Hart introduces the idea of a predictive theory. It could be urged that he was concerned to explain not the internal and external aspects of rule, but merely two kinds of motivation, both applicable to the internal aspect, that is to say, motivation springing from rule-guidance, and motivation springing from a prediction on the part of the person concerned of what might happen to him on his not obeying the rule. And indeed there are men and women, perhaps defective in their moral disposition, who could take such a view. In this sense one might truly speak of the approach being predictive. It seems however that Hart is concerned not with the

14

actor, in these circumstances, but with the observer and what he chooses to observe, whether it be the causal relationship between the traffic lights being red and the cars stopping or whether it be the manner and the circumstances in which the driver of the car experienced an obligation to stop. Predictive in the first case raises an expectation that we can identify such regularities in social phenomena that the existence of one will give rise to the other much in the way this occurs in the natural sciences, and with the same inevitability.

It is necessary to ask however if the social sciences in general rely on a predictive theory understood in this manner. One could perhaps point to some of the early theorists of the social sciences, indeed some of the builders of modern European thought, who certainly at first sight appeared to take such a view. If Auguste Comte was the first writer to use the term sociology, he also used the term social physics, understandably perhaps if we accept that 'the philosophical principle of the science (is) that social phenomena are subject to natural laws admitting of rational prevision.'[8] There is much in Comte that is implausible to the modern mind, but his influence was considerable, not least on J.S. Mill who popularised his work in Britain, and to whom we can trace the fashion in the social sciences of seeking and validating generalisations which are causal in character, that is to say, which provide a basis for causal explanations. In this manner, it is claimed, one is tempted into a mimicry of the physical sciences, into an expectation of a mechanical regularity in social phenomena between cause and event, which, if it is at times uncertain, is uncertain not by reason of any defect in the theory but rather by reason of the difficulty in data collection and interpretation.

Insofar as modern social science relies on this approach it is indeed based on predictive theory of some kind, and Hart's concern is justifed. But is it so based? There are many social scientists who would find the presentation at best somewhat simplistic and while questioning the influence today in such matters of Comte or Mill or indeed even of Weber and Durkheim, would also go on to say that we can take too simplistic a view as well of the rather complex explorations of these men. After all we must

15

distinguish[9] between 'laws' understood as causal, predictive and inevitable, and trends which, however influential, are subject to modification; and much of the so-called laws outlined by these early writers, reveal themselves, under closer examination, to be trends, that is, ultimately subject to modification, for otherwise their very political passions and purposes would be meaningless. Or, even in a less exacting way, scholars may be concerned with trends which derive from historical sequences and indeed causalities, which are not urged as a basis for prediction, but when viewed with hindsight have great explanatory power.

But there is much ambiguity here because when we speak of such trends we may have in mind that there are currents in events which prompt the setting of a particular course or we may see in them a reflection of a direct and inevitable causal chain, which although real and predictable is difficult if not impossible adequately to descry. In such latter circumstances whether we speak of trends or of causal laws, the nature of the observation is the same, the two differing not in kind but in the degree of exactitude and comprehension which is currently available. I believe that this second understanding of trends lies at the base of the social sciences, and therefore we may properly continue to explore it in its more exacting form of direct causality.

It is a position which is not without some philosophical justification. We must remind ourselves that men are natural phenomena and are subject to certain natural laws, such as going grey, becoming sick and dying. In regard to such matters one can of course establish certain statistical laws, although they are not directly applicable to the individual; but in a more precise sense there are natural laws as well which appear to govern individual lives. Indeed the whole business of medicine is in large part derived from the study of a man as a natural phenomenon.

We can be confronted, then, with all the causal connections which we see in the physical sciences, more complex perhaps by reason of the complexity of man's nature, more limited in their application in certain areas than in others, but validly existing. All this seems reasonable enough. But some philosophers of the social sciences will go further and say that whether we speak of man as a

16

natural phenomenon or as a social phenomenon, one is influenced by the other, often the distinction is blurred and impossible to maintain, the reason being that we are speaking of a single reality whether it be social or natural. True, social configurations are not objective in the sense that the rain-clouds are, or mountains or forests but neither are they subjective like dreams or flights of fancy. They are, as most social scientists would concede at the theoretical level, 'intersubjective constructions.'[10] But it would be highly implausible to suggest that because they participate in a different form of objective reality they are not subject to the same inevitable laws, although often immensely difficult to identify, which govern the natural world. It is for this reason that certain social scientists will say that Hart's criticism of predictive theory is based on a far too radical disconnection between social and physical phenomena.

There is another, less fundamental, approach to the question of some inevitable causal chain. The economist, for example, in attempting to explain the market, will see the buyer and the seller not as persons but as categories. He can in these circumstances attribute to the category such characteristics as appear to him to be appropriate, for example that, *ceteris paribus*, the buyer should wish to buy at the lowest price available. This is intended to correspond to the economist's experience in the actual business of buying and selling but it is not claimed that it reflects it in all its aspects. However, it is an assumption of behaviour that the economist builds in, and therefore, for the purposes of the particular model of the world that he is developing, it can be taken as a datum. In these circumstances the dilemmas of rule-guidance such as the buyer may actually experience are not relevant to him except in so far as they result in such regularities of behaviour that they can, with plausibility, be built into the model. He can go further and devise other categories in relation to the market to which he can also attribute characteristics, often resulting in great sophistications both of the categories and of their relationships. Now what emerges is a model which is entirely rational and in which causality is indeed of the mechanical kind, not because the world is so but because the model built by the economist is. This of course is not a literal description of a market, but a model of one, and its value lies in using it as a measure.

Insofar as a real market corresponds to it then, it raises strong presumptions that certain consequences will follow. It provides therefore a basis for strategic planning. If the deviance of one of the factors making up the model were to create a sharp disequilibrium, for example, then a corresponding deviance in the actual market would invite remedy. Economics understood in this rather simplified way, it is suggested, (and it is certainly not the only way in which economics is understood) is not primarily an explanation of society but a tool for governing it (which is perhaps the reason why economists, more than other social scientists, tend to describe their calling as a profession rather than an area of scholarship).

It might be suggested therefore that social scientists who engage in model building or variations of it avoid any necessary commitment to a mechanical notion of causality, except in respect of their own intellectual construction. But this too runs into difficulty because the logic of the model ultimately is taken to reflect the logic of the social phenomena themselves and their relationships, because otherwise the model could not act as an instrument of explication.

How then should we, at this point in the argument, see the social sciences? Although one is not engaged in a misleading mimicry of the natural sciences, although frequently cause and effect seem to be related on some conceptual level rather than the physical, nevertheless social scientists see themselves characteristically as scientists relying on some fundamental and necessary order in the world which is capable of being empirically observed and its laws comprehended even if only partially.

Hart, of course, would claim that the notion of obligation cannot be delineated by this approach since, as we have seen, the scientific external observer is concerned with his own scientifically determined criteria, the criteria he can himself identify, while the notion of obligation and the notion of rule-guidance require us to take account of the subject's criteria, as well as the observer's, indeed at times primarily.[11] But while there may be limits to the uses of scientific investigation, it clearly has a great deal to offer.

18

Why then, it may be asked, should not both systems of inquiry, the external and the internal be used, one reinforcing the other? Why should there not be an approach which at one and the same time permits the observing of and the giving meaning to external regularities, and offers a place of equal value to the views of those observed? Now Hart claims that there is a sense in which the first drives out the second and this is the crux of the matter.[12] Other writers would take a less dramatic view and even Durkheim in his study of the laws of society saw the 'external fact' primarily as symbolic of the internal, the moral, phenomenon which must be seen as the superior reality.[13]

But there is much to be said for Hart's view. There are certain assumptions lying behind the scientific method which put it into a mode of intolerance. It is assumed in some sense that true and reliable knowledge emerges out of scientific practices in a manner which is automatic. Further, as we have already noted, truth is regarded as single, and if one combines these two points then the object of science must be to eliminate argument and uncertainty, and in a word to eliminate the point of view urged by Hart. Because Hart does not adopt the so called scientific method (although his method is one of logical analysis) there is much in his statement that while the scientific method excludes his perspective, the contrary is not necessarily the case.

This apparent imperiousness of the scientific method (and I do not use the term in any pejorative way) is of the greatest importance because of the manner in which it appears to exclude some traditional forms of scholarship. It therefore deserves some further illustration and this we can find in the work of Allan Flanders, one of the most influential of the British theorists in industrial relations. At first sight he appears, as Hart does, to set rule-guidance at the very centre of his theoretical position. He sees, in a manner similar to that of John Dunlop,[14] the process of industrial relations and in particular of collective bargaining as resulting in rules, indeed a web of rules. However, he understands the nature of rule guidance in a very different way.

His discussion in *Management and Unions*[15] and particularly the well known chapter which attempts a theoretical analysis of collective bargaining is for the purpose of disconnecting collective bargaining from the notion of a market and attaching it instead to the notion of a political system, and for these purposes, while he sees the making of an individual employment agreement as a market-type economic bargain, he sees the collective agreement between the trade union and the employer as an agreement on the rules which will govern the individual agreement and therefore in its intrinsic character a political rather than an economic activity.[16]

We shall take up later Flanders' notion of a market — which in my view must not be seen as a simple, rather anarchic, arena within which self-interest is pursued, but instead very much a rule-determined matter, as modern scholarship tends to emphasise; and these rules may be bargained for as much as any other element. Our major purpose here however is to explore the method by which Flanders approached the problem. He spoke about two systems, an economic system and a political system. In this kind of approach, a system is identified first and then used as an explanatory programme. Such systems are logically distinct as we shall see and therefore compete with one another as explanatory programmes. They are in that sense mutually exclusive. This is the reason why the notion of economic and the notion of political cannot be intermingled in a manner which at first sight seems self-evident; this is what provides Flanders with his dilemma. Let us consider why this is so.

We saw earlier that there were three areas to which in some sense we accorded reality. There were the natural phenomena, trees, mountains and clouds and also of course men. There were what were described as social realities, intersubjective realities, such as nations, golf clubs and trade unions; and there were also models, abstract intellectual structures, such as a market. Now a system, as described by Flanders, is closest to the last. It is distinguished from the second, from a nation or a trade union, by the fact that it is, in Dunlop's phrase,[17] logically an abstraction. Logic here is the key to the idea, because logicality and logical relationships can be achieved only by the attributing of characteristics to the model which are predictable and mutually consistent. A man then, a buyer or a seller, is, as we have seen in the economic model of the market, not a natural person but a category to which characteristics are attributed which approximate to the natural world but which must lie consistently within the model and which therefore must be predictable. In an economic model certain characteristics are assumed which are not the same as those in a political model. But since each model must be wholly consistent internally, these cannot be seen as interesting variations in the same model but wholly exclusive systems. This then was the reason for Flanders' difficulty with economic as against political systems. But from our point of view, although he discusses rules and sees them as central, they are central to a system which requires not a consideration of a natural man reflecting on those things that guide him, their origin, their legitimacy and their binding force but rather a consideration of a system where categories are created and characteristics attributed to them which derive essentially from external observation.[18]

It appears therefore that it is somewhat unprofitable to start with the notion of a system, as Flanders has done, since it leads one into all the difficulties described by Herbert Hart. Instead we must attempt to understand activities in the industrial relations field as patterns of freedoms and obligation, some being similar to the freedoms and obligations of what men describe as a market, others not.

I am therefore driven to two conclusions. I am driven to the view that externally observed regularities of a causal or quasi-causal kind appear to lead away from, not towards, the essence of rule as Hart described it, that which forms the basis for claims and demands, for admissions, criticisms, and punishment. All the significant aspects of rule, understood in this way, cannot be seen by observation of external regularities. The notion of obligation cannot be successfully reached in this way and it is my belief that the notion of obligation and its exploration are fundamental to the study of industrial relations. Secondly, I am driven to the view that the scientific method as frequently pursued in the social sciences requires of one intellectually an exclusive commitment. We cannot pursue it wholeheartedly and at the same time admit those more juridical considerations which lie at the basis of Hart's presentation.

Before going on to consider a little more fully why we should regard obligation as being of such importance for our study, let me recognise too that in the discussion so far I have by no means presented the social sciences comprehensively. There are for example anthropologists whose methods I have not reviewed and indeed one is very conscious of the fact that much of the scholarly work in the field of industrial relations could be described as industrial anthropology. Nor can one offer anything but admiration at the growing skill and sophistication of data-garnering. Nevertheless I believe Hart identified correctly the governing trend within them and it is this governing trend that I have found, at least for industrial relations, to be inadequate.

3

The notion of obligation is the notion of a context, that is to say it implies a constraint (although perhaps a creative constraint) on one's activity. In order to understand the character of the context, the character of the pattern of constraints, it is necessary to dwell first on the activity itself.

There is an assumption in a civilized society, which we must take as axiomatic, that a man in his actions is free. Essentially he may do as he wishes. However there are constraints, some deriving from his own status as a man (and the expectations which society has of him as a consequence)[19] but, for our purposes, deriving in particular from the obligations he owes to others. Now these obligations in turn are the correlatives of the rights which these others possess. But the rights are inert; they justify the obligations which constrain a man's freedom; they are not themselves active. Moreover, while there is a clear correlation between a right and a duty, essentially because they tend to be different aspects of the same relationship, no such correlation exists between freedom as an activity and the occasional obligations which constrain it and which spring from the rights of others. In a word the notion of free activity, an essentially dynamic concept, must be distinguished from the equally important but inert concept of a right. Even in countries such as Ireland which have a written constitution, one finds frequently confusion regarding rights and freedoms despite the efforts of certain scholars to try to clarify the ideas that lie behind them.[20] For example, in 1978 an Irish High Court judge in a case where teachers, in a dispute with school authorities, refused to enrol school children said: 'The character of an act depends on the circumstances in which it is done and the exercise of a constitutional right for the purpose of infringing the constitutional rights of others is an abuse of that right which in my opinion can be restrained by the courts'.[21] This could well lead to the notion of conflicting constitutional rights, the problem of adjudicating between them, and even the possibility of some hierarchy of value in their regard but this — in my view — quite false opposition is avoided if, in expressing the problem, we do so by contrasting the freedom of the teachers to work or to cease to work with the obligation they owed, among other things, to the children not to deprive them of their right to educational opportunity. In a word it was a question of the exercise of a freedom within certain constraints.

It is not surprising that this difficulty should arise in judicial evaluations. A judicial decision is made between two parties in regard to their relationship. It is the relationship between the parties, not the activity of one party or the other, that is explored and since neither one party nor the other, *qua* party, is the focus, it follows that the freedoms and rights are seen in a static way, and are therefore readily open to confusion. When however we come to consider industrial relations we must see it all in some dynamic sense; we must see the workers, the trade union or the employer primarily in the role of an actor, occasionally confronted with obligations which he either resolves or conflicts with. In these circumstances the distinction between freedom and right is of the greatest importance and the examination of obligation must be seen in that context as well. This is the reason too why in this approach we are not concerned with law as a curial practice. We are concerned not with *lex* primarily but with *jus*. The discipline we pursue is the discipline of jurisprudence, understood in the English, not in the French, use of that term, jurisprudence which

23

stems from a consciousness of personal obligation and the extent of its legitimacy but always springing from the person seeing himself as an actor within the industrial environment.

We may summarise the position therefore as follows. In order fully to understand the notion of obligation for our purposes, it is necessary to have regard to the actor and not to the adjudicator, to have regard to the person in his actions experiencing the implications of rule-guidance, rather than to the person reflecting on the relationship which might exist between two persons in contention. We must understand freedom, right and obligation not in a judgemental sense but in an experiential sense.

But how are we to understand an actor in these circumstances? There are moral philosophers[22] who take the view that for an understanding of justice we must understand the idea of the other, that is to say, the idea that because a person is a human person he possesses rights which we may not contravene irrespective of the error which we believe him to be in; and logically therefore no matter how profoundly wrongheaded he appears to us, no matter how impatient, indeed outraged we are regarding his views, we must none the less, particularly if we are the stronger, create those institutions which are essential in order that his rights as a person should be protected against our impatience. The Rawlsian[23] view of justice is a variation of this although the earlier position appears to me to be somewhat more elegant. One way or the other, however, the point is made.

Such a view is quite a hardheaded one. It does not deny the intensity of feeling one possesses in respect of one's own cause. It can accommodate quite readily the idea that neither the employer nor the trade union pursues, as a primary objective, the notion of industrial peace. Each one in fact pursues his own interest. Only those concerned with the preservation of the relationship, that is, only those who see themselves in some sense as adjudicators, place the notion of harmony in the relationship above the other objectives. The parties however see industrial peace as a desirable condition within which they can achieve their objectives but not itself the overriding objective at all times.

In saying this we have done two things. We have validated the notion of the pursuit of self-interest and we have (in the earlier paragraph) validated as well the need to pursue that self-interest within a context of obligation which springs necessarily from the nature of what is generally taken to be a just society.

There is a final point, a consideration of the fruitfulness of this approach. We have already suggested that it reflects in very large measure the preoccupations of those engaged in industrial relations and therefore, in a general way, assists in clarification. This can be developed further by recognising, how, in our consideration of obligation, we identify more clearly the important concept of legitimacy. Before an obligation is felt as being in some way compelling, it must be seen to be legitimate, that is to say, the rule that lies behind it must be accepted as being a real and compelling basis. In all areas of disputation, and in a particularly self-evident way in industrial relations, there are occasions where there is no rule that one can look to for guidance. This is particularly so when we are dealing with substantive, rather than procedural, matters. Traditionally in the study of industrial relations such disputes are called disputes as to interest, of which disputes in relation to wage claims are by far the best known example. We propose to discuss such disputes at greater length in chapter II. On the other hand there may be a dispute in respect of which rule-guidance is perfectly appropriate but where the rule itself or its application may come under challenge.

The difference therefore between the parties may be because of the absence of any rule on which obligation can be erected or it may be because obligation is differently understood. More than that, convention tends to change over time creating conflict where there was once consensus and not only between large and differentiated groups but even from one group to another within the same employment. This too we shall consider in chapter II.

The exploration of legitimacy therefore, provides a basis for an understanding of what can in other circumstances appear to be a minefield of conflicting ideas, but it also provides wide scope for empirical research guided by a very precise and exacting idea of what kind of information is necessary.

4

Let us at this stage attempt some categorisation of the various obligations which an employer and his organisation, an employee and his collectivity and indeed the public authority itself (seen as an actor in the field) may experience in conducting their affairs, that is to say, in acting within the industrial relations environment.

Perhaps the best way to approach it would be to identify as the three major categories the following: those obligations which limit the actor by reason of agreements, conventions or custom, those obligations which spring from personal rights (whether fundamental or statutory) which others possess, and finally those obligations which spring from the intervention of the public authority. In chapter II we take up the first of these categories, perhaps the most ambiguous and uncertain of the three.

CHAPTER TWO

Obligations arising from Agreements

1

In this section we deal with the obligations owed by reason of agreement, convention or custom. We shall try to approach the discussion from the point of view of the different actors, but before doing so it is necessary to clarify further the manner in which obligation arises in these circumstances. As we have already seen, obligation is conceptually secondary to free activity, to the pursuit of self-interest or group-interest, and this must be explored first. For our purposes, the arena of this activity is the employment market and the activity itself, being the pursuit of a group interest rather than self-interest, is usually described as collective bargaining.

We have seen that Allan Flanders[1] wished to exclude from such collective negotiation the notion of a bargain, the notion of a market-type activity, on the grounds that, since the object of collective bargaining was rule-making, the activity was more properly a political one. An exploration of this view of Flanders' will help us greatly in clarifying the issue.

The term collective bargaining is probably one of the most frequently used in industrial relations. It raises the analogy of an individual bargain in the employment market and is normally understood to have the same characteristics as an individual bargain, the difference merely being that the parties, or perhaps one of them, the workers, are collectivities. It is this point that Flanders challenges. He regards it as a persistent source of confusion in understanding and evaluating the social institution which the term was meant to describe. Collective bargaining, he claims, is not analogous to individual bargaining. An agreement between an individual worker and his employer he sees as indeed a bargain; a collective agreement is not. Instead it is a rule-making

27

process and this he regards as being a feature which has no proper counterpart in individual bargaining. His principal point therefore is that since the negotiation is not about the employment of a particular person but instead about the rules governing that employment it cannot be a bargain.

He offers other reasons. He suggests that the relationship between a trade union and an employer is a power relationship between organisations, analogous to the diplomatic use of power and therefore a political and not an economic process. And finally he makes what are on the whole rather obscure points about the authorship of the rules and their administration. The major argument on which he rests however appears to be that the object of the negotiation is rule-making and not direct employment. In a word the argument is that the object of the negotiation determines whether we should describe the activity as bargaining or not.

One might ask at the outset why, in a matter such as this, one should distinguish between bargaining on the introduction of a procedural rule and bargaining on an issue of substance. Both surely are bargains. It occurs to one that terms of supply, for example, decided on between a purchaser and a supplier, are procedural rules in a fully analogous way in that they relate not to the goods supplied but to the manner of their supply. These are quite commonly subject to a bargain. Contrariwise, there is also some implication in the view advanced by Flanders that an individual making a bargain of employment somehow enters a situation where there are no rules. Let us recognise a point which we shall have occasion to develop, that is, that every market is in fact rule-governed; it is the nature of the market that it should be so. And if we were to make a distinction between the individual employment bargain and a collective bargain it would rather be a distinction between different points on a continuum. The rules that govern the individual bargain (for example, the standard pay) are indeed rules which are determined by the collective bargain, but at the level of the collective bargain these rules were issues upon which agreement was sought, but this agreement in turn was sought in the context of earlier rules either agreed between the parties or in a larger negotiating arena. Once the point is grasped that a rule, prior to its being negotiated, is in its essential character an issue, much of the difficulty is resolved.

Nevertheless our problem may here be a question of definition. It may well be that Flanders wishes to confine the word bargain to those objectives that are essentially economic in character. In developing the point, he remarks on a trade union's objective of limiting the number entering the employment market or the objective of determining the minimum wage within a monopoly supply situation. He says of these activities that they are characteristically non-market, non-competitive. But the distinction is a fine one. If I limit the number entering the employment market, is it not analogous to my limiting the supply of goods in a monopoly situation, thereby influencing the market? And if I determine the minimum wage within a monopoly supply situation, is it not in fact a form of retail price maintenance? Perhaps the point might be made in justification of Flanders' position that bargaining should be applied only to those activities which are legitimate in the market place and not to those which distort the activity. It might be suggested that a limitation of supply and a distortion of price are seen in the matter of goods (services are not so clear an example) as being intrinsically wrong because price is the major if not the sole nexus. But this too provides us with a difficulty. Bodies that engage in such activities are no less seen to be involved, however improperly, in a market activity. But apart from that there are numerous market rules which are considered necessary to the operation of the market as a competitive activity and which in no sense are seen to distort it. Those rules which are intended to limit the influence of a dominant supplier or a dominant purchaser are cases in point.

It appears then that we must accommodate both negotiation on the issue and negotiation on the rules which may govern it, and the latter both as an issue for negotiation and as a source of obligation. We have already taken account of the difficulty Flanders found himself in because of the manner of his approach, the establishment of two mutually exclusive models, the economic system and the political system. We however, in our approach, encounter no such difficulty. We can therefore securely accept the idea of a market

29

with the implications which we will now explore as long as we are clear that in using the term bargaining whether in the case of an individual job seeker or in the case of collective negotiation, we are concerned with rule no less than with issue.

2

From this and from earlier considerations of Flanders, what can we say about this area of activity, an area that accommodates such ideas as a labour market, contracts of personal employment, collective bargaining and also the continuing personal relationships within the work situation?

In accordance with our general approach, we shall view the area as observers within, as observers experiencing the thrust of self-interest which we see as a primary freedom, but limited by the obligations we owe to others. (In speaking of self-interest, we are not speaking of selfishness but rather the pursuit of personally determined objectives which might indeed be selfish but might also in their nature be models of philanthropy.) We have already recognised that in such a situation there are issues that are governed by rule, and there are issues that are not; there are issues where an adjudication can be made by reference to a rule and there are issues where no adjudication between right and wrong is possible, where in fact the notion of right and wrong does not exist.

Let us explore the second area first, since it is the heartland of disputation. It is an area where a bargain has not yet been made, where the agreement from which the obligations will spring has not yet been determined. It is, in a word, the process of bargaining rather than the consequences of the bargain. In a simple market situation, I, as a buyer, will attempt, *ceteris paribus,* to buy at the lowest price. That is where my interest lies. The vendor, on his part, will, *ceteris paribus,* attempt to sell at the highest price. That is where his interest lies. Both of us are free to engage in this activity, subject to the obligations we owe to others (which, we have seen, spring from the rights with which they are possessed) but there is a further constraint which in a market situation is far more

30

significant; it is the constraint which arises from the fact that both I and the vendor must, if we are to conclude a bargain or a resolution of our differences, accommodate the interests of the other. There is no rule that we should; neither is there a rule, such as splitting the difference, to which we can have recourse as a regulator. It is a simple question of accommodation.

The second characteristic in a bargain is this. The encounter must take place for both parties in one and the same arena, in which the money nexus is an essential part, otherwise the notion of mutual constraint and mutual accommodation does not arise. The third characteristic is that the bargaining takes place within a context of rule, within a context of mutual obligation. The more simple the encounter (that is, the more it is concerned with the money nexus merely and not with any other relationship between the parties) the more elementary are the rules that govern it. If I purchase a newspaper from a newsvendor, my relationship with him need be only the most casual, the nexus being the offer of the precise sum which the purchase of a newspaper requires, but even here the encounter is not without rules, some significant (I am for example prohibited from deliberately and misleadingly offering the wrong price), some merely conventional such as the obligations of courtesy. They are however of a very elementary kind. But if the encounter occurs in a societal setting, as when a group of traders continuously deal with one another, then the societal requirements themselves are imposed on the bargaining relationship, resulting in a growth of obligation, one to another, and consequently, in the bargain itself, a greater complexity of rule, even to the point where the actual bargaining encounter may become obscured. The trading in personal services rather than goods is more complex still, but at the apex of this hierarchy of complexity one must place the employment function.

A firm is a society of people, diversified in their activities, but with a common purpose. This is its settled character. It follows from this that conflicts, when they arise, are necessarily exceptional; if it were not so, then the firm could not survive. The relationship therefore between an employer and an employee is normally a cooperative one. It is true that diverse interests are clearly present

31

to a greater or lesser degree at the point of first employment where a bargain of some kind must be made. Furthermore, during the course of the employment diverse interests arise in a wholly legitimate manner from time to time, where, for example, the employee seeks a higher wage, or where the employer proposes to introduce machinery which threatens job security. But all this is in the context of a common cooperative endeavour.

The point about collective bargaining however is this: it is called into play only at the point of a diversity of interest, and only when the workers as a collectivity are involved. This is what gives a workers' collectivity, a trade union, its essentially adversary character. When the workers wish to cast themselves institutionally in a cooperative role, the trade union, although often expressing goodwill, and often indeed seeking such a development, finds it difficult to express such a function by means of its own institutional form, because of its explicitly adversarial character, and as a practical consequence, participative collectivities tend to be distinguished from trade union collectivities.[2] It could be urged that in our industrial society, unlike some others, the adversary role of the collectivity is too powerfully organised and that manifestly cooperative matters are converted into adversarial issues. There is much truth in such a criticism. The point we must make however is that while the bargaining function, that which concerns the adversarial issue, may be obscured deeply in the day-to-day functioning of the firm, it is still an essential part of its conduct, but one which, as we have come to recognise, will necessarily be conducted within an extensive and diverse context of rule.[3]

We now go on to recognise that in the process of bargaining there are different interests at work, interests which, if a dispute is in prospect, are in substantial conflict; but we must also recognise that, as a rule, each interest is quite legitimate. By legitimate we mean not that which is legal but rather that which is seen to be generally acceptable. There was a view, extraordinarily persistent among common law lawyers, that an attempt by trade unions to oblige a common rate of pay was unlawful as a conspiracy in restraint of trade,[4] but such an activity now is seen as being wholly legitimate. Equally, the desire of the employer to resist a wage

32

demand is also seen as legitimate, and any attempt by a trade union to oblige additional payments from an employer by way of penalty for not conceding more readily tends to be strongly resisted as was clear from the attitude of the Minister for Labour in the 1970 banks' dispute.[5] Even when a bargain has been made, it is not necessarily seen as a concession to some objectively determined correct position but rather an accommodation which does not invade a party's view of where its best interest actually lies.

But if there are conflicting interests, there is no less a powerful impetus at times towards successful accommodation in a manner which does as little damage as possible to the interests involved. And it is this characteristic, this impetus for accommodation, that leads us to an understanding of the institutions that are developed as a consequence. It is true that there are some market situations where the need for the parties to reach an accommodation with one another is not particularly great. If my newsvendor chooses to raise arbitrarily the price of a particular journal (which he would be highly unlikely to do), I am free to go elsewhere and feel therefore no great pressure to reach an accommodation with him. Clearly however a wage claim arises in a very different situation, within an arena already rich in inter-relationships which makes some ultimate accommodation between the parties essential.

These are the circumstances of our study and it is clear that at the very outset they raise as a problem the question of bargaining power and the equality, or lack of it, of the parties in that regard. We have already seen that Flanders[6] regarded this power relationship as critical, causing him to present it as yet another reason for seeing collective bargaining as a political activity primarily. And there have been many sociologists of industrial relations who see as the central theme of industrial relations this question of the power of the parties to compel. Certainly the question of bargaining power is of considerable importance in this area of the discussion. In a modern industrial society, however, it does not always, or even frequently, result in the overriding of one party by the other. The parties tend to reach accommodation in other ways. In gross cases, an employer, feeling himself to be greatly oppressed, may retire from that business activity altogether, and equally workers, treated in a like manner, will perhaps seek to leave the employment. However, in general one finds, in such circumstances, appeal to independent institutions. While it would appear that an appeal to a third party in such disputes as to interest (as they are frequently called)[7] arises at times because of some desire for equity between unequal bargaining parties, the device itself has also been availed of with great frequency by parties broadly equal in their bargaining power, largely because, locked in an inescapable relationship which requires them to reach an accommodation, they find such a device vastly superior to a demonstration of power by means of a strike, lock-out or other form of industrial action.

This third party reference is of the greatest importance to us in our exploration of the nature of a bargaining relationship since it provides us with a window into the nature of the relationship itself. We have been careful up to this point to avoid the use of any term which might imply some form of adjudication because, in a word, we have no rule in respect of which an adjudication can be made. Instead, as we have been careful to emphasise, we see interests in conflict, each lawful as far as it goes, and a desire for some accommodation. On the other hand, if there were a rule to be applied one could anticipate a different kind of third party response, not a third party offering, as it were, a third view, but an adjudication, a judgement, which derives its legitimacy from the existence of the rule. This distinction is of the greatest importance and we shall discuss it more fully in a moment. Our purpose here however is to underline the significance of the third party reference. Its character helps us to identify whether we are dealing with a matter of rule or whether we are dealing with a conflict of interest.

We began our discussion on third party reference by considering the plight of an unequal partner in the bargain and it is not inappropriate that we should proceed in this way developing first the implications of inequality of bargaining power and moving on to consider the elements in a situation where there is broad equality between the parties. Under the Industrial Relations Act 1946, workers in general were given access to the Labour Court but civil servants and similar employees were excluded[8] apparently on the

34

grounds that their inclusion might invite them to take a view of their relationship with their employer, the government, which would be excessively and improperly adversarial in character. At that time, civil servants for a number of reasons found it inconceivable that they should enter into industrial conflict with the government on employment issues and not uncommonly found themselves treated in a summary and very casual fashion by the Department of Finance, which had overall responsibility for personnel matters in the civil service. It was in these circumstances that the civil service associations and unions sought what they described as a scheme of conciliation and arbitration and this, by reason of the special political prominence of one of their leaders,[9] was conceded in 1950. The arbitration process was seen as the centrepiece of the system, providing for a jointly appointed independent arbitrator, explicitly temporary in character, who would offer a view on the dispute argued before him, his formal position being chairman of a jointly established board but in practice the sole effective voice. The consequence was that no matter how small a civil service association was or how minor its claim it could oblige the civil service establishment officers (as the personnel officers were known) to appear before an independent arbitrator, to argue a case out in detail and to have publicly promulgated the arbitrator's decision.

The key point in this disparate bargaining situation, the point that gave a promise of equity, was the powerful sense in which the arbitrator's decision was seen to be conclusive. This was not of course provided for in the scheme. No government could lightly accept such an obligation, since exchequer considerations of a substantial kind could be involved in an arbitration decision affecting the civil service as a whole, and it was provided therefore that a government could quite legitimately, on receiving the decision of the arbitrator, refer the matter to parliament with a recommendation that the award be varied or rejected. So powerful however was the commitment on the part of the civil servants to the idea of an indefeasible award that when, in 1952, the government chose to refer a particular award to parliament for review, there were vehement charges of a breach of faith, not indeed sustainable

35

under the terms of the agreement on conciliation and arbitration, but springing from the civil servants' view of the essential nature of such an understanding if their weakness as a bargaining partner were to be remedied to any degree.[10]

The idea of creating an independent arbitration scheme, the arbitrator being agreed and holding office for a brief period, associated with the idea of an award that was indefeasible, began to be applied to a great number of other groups as well who either because of their intrinsic weakness or their reluctance to engage in industrial action required such a device. In more recent times it has been extended to the police and to small specialised groups such as chief executive officers of Vocational Education Committees in whom industrial action would be seen either to be civilly wrong or in practical terms impossible. Even in the case of a large union, where equality in bargaining strength is not seen as a problem, one finds many instances where arbitration is not unwelcome. Quite apart from a practical need to reach a peaceful accommodation there is also the fact that disputes vary greatly in the extent to which they gain support from membership and consequently support for industrial action, and implicitly bargaining power can in certain circumstances be surprisingly slight even for a union normally of considerable strength. We find a recognition of the need for such arbitration procedures in the recommendations of the first Employer Labour Conference in 1962. During its brief life[11] a number of joint sub-committees was established, one dealing with negotiation procedure, and this sub-committee recommended some form of binding arbitration in a number of limited instances, where for example the subject matter of dispute was not of great importance or where only one or a small number of workers was involved. In the event the executive council of Congress were not prepared to accept the recommendation in that form (although they accepted the recommendations of the other three sub-committees), and this I suspect arose primarily because the understanding of what was meant by importance could in any event be a matter of some dispute and secondly, there were many instances where cases concerning one or a small number of workers had inflamed a whole employment. But nevertheless the purpose

36

was obvious enough and had considerable acceptance. Clearly the kind of disputes under contemplation normally did not receive widespread support and therefore the bargaining effectiveness of the trade union would necessarily be limited. Of course, there were other reasons as well, but it is important to recognise how bargaining effectiveness may shift from one instance to another, and therefore new institutions of this conclusive kind, based on independent arbitration, could be called into being, which although conclusive were not adjudicatory in character.

Let us glance, in this context, at the Labour Court. While the Court can provide an arbitration service, its typical function is to engage in an enquiry and issue a recommendation to the parties. This is not a binding arbitration in any sense, although good industrial relations practice would indicate that it should be given considerable status. Trade unions and employers, who are in no sense unequal in their bargaining strength, frequently have recourse to the Court in the hope that such recourse would break an impasse which in other circumstances could deteriorate into a conflict which would damage both parties.

That the recommendation of the Labour Court is essentially a third view and not a judgement, that is to say, not dependent on rule, is clear from the Labour Court's own account of itself. The Act of 1946 did of course attempt to set out criteria which the Court should adopt in making recommendations, but these were found to be somewhat confusing and contradictory in that they asked the Court to look to the public interest, to the promoting of industrial peace, to the notion of fairness and to the prospect of the terms being acceptable to the parties.[12] The first chairman of the Court, R.J.P. Mortished, writing in 1947 said for example:[13]

> Unfortunately for the Court it may not be easy to reconcile all four of the considerations which it has in mind; a settlement acceptable to the parties might be against the public interest and one which was not acceptable to the parties would hardly promote industrial peace. The Court must solve this problem as best it can in the circumstances of each dispute; it cannot take the easy course of applying a hard and fast rule to all sorts of cases.

Indeed more than that the Court, particularly in the 1960s when national pay settlements were in the air, tended to resist strongly the idea that it should be cast in the role of a promoter or implementer of such agreements. It took the view, instead, perhaps in too simple a way, that the Court should be free to seek a settlement as best it could in all the circumstances of the case, taking account of course of the need for consistency and taking account of the national interest whether expressed in national bargains or not, but ultimately being free to pursue, in common sense, what seemed to be appropriate for a solution of the dispute actually under examination. This view indeed seems to have influenced the amendment to the 1941 Act[14] which, in 1969, provided that:

> The Court, having investigated a trade dispute, may make a recommendation setting forth its opinion on the merits of the dispute and the terms on which it should be settled.

The decade of the 1970s was preeminently a decade of highly centralised pay bargaining which required of the Labour Court some adjudicatory function in relation to the agreements, and in addition it was given explicit judicial functions in relation to the Anti-discrimination (Pay) Act 1974 and the Employment Equality Act 1977. This has led to some confusion and some general if uncertain recognition that there are at least two quite distinct functions involved here, the offer of a third view to parties attempting to accommodate one another in a bargain, and the exercise of a judgement in relation to the private law of an agreement already existing between the parties or the public law of a statute against which an offence may have been committed. But the function of promoting an accommodation, so continuously asserted, is not in any sense excluded.

When a third party is engaged in promoting an accommodation between those in dispute, it clearly cannot enforce its view or even claim that, in offering the view, it is relying on the application of some governing rule. There is a persistent desire on the part of some to see conferred on the Labour Court or a similar body some ability to oblige enforcement by the imposition of penalty in precisely these areas of bargain and accommodation. For example the Commission of Enquiry on Industrial Relations recommended[15] that where there was dispute as to recognition or where

38

there was a dispute between unions, then the parties could have recourse to a Labour Relations Board, with an appeal to a Labour Relations Court, but this, it was recommended, was to be the only procedure open to them. Industrial action which might follow would not have the protection of the 1906 Trade Disputes Act and an employer could seek remedies in the courts of law. This recommendation has not been implemented and it is unlikely to be. Its impropriety, however, springs primarily from a confusion of categories, a failure to recognise that what we are dealing with here are two parties legitimately seeking each its own advantage and failing to find an accommodation. Neither, in the pursuit of its activities, is as yet breaching its obligation to any other party. In a word, no rights are involved and no law is applicable.

While the institutions we have described are therefore of the greatest importance, they are not judicial in their procedures, they merely promote accommodation. If they have compelling power, it is only because the parties so bind themselves in advance (and they need not do so), not because of any intrinsic legitimacy for such a purpose in the institutions themselves. At best they are persuasive and therefore can never invite a penalty.

3

Let us now move to the second major area, the area of constraints, the area where an actor in the pursuit of his activity is confronted with the obligations he owes to others. Later we shall go on to discuss obligations deriving from antecedent personal rights and from the public interest. For the moment, however, we are concerned with those obligations which derive from the bargain, whether written and precise or broad and consensual.

Let us consider the most straightforward case, a formal collective agreement between a trade union and an employer. It is of course in every sense an agreement, but — and this is its special characteristic — it appears in practice to differ from other agreements in the important area of legal sanctions. In the ordinary course of business, if I, having entered into a contract, find the other party in breach of the arrangement, I can seek a remedy in the courts where, in general, the principle is that I should be entitled to restoration in regard to the damage and loss suffered by me. This principle applies to a trade union as well where it is concerned in what one might describe as a personal agreement, that is to say, one in which the trade union acts in a manner similar to a natural person, in buying a house for example or employing staff. In a word such bargains are normally justiciable in the ordinary way, although there are certain statutory limitations.[16] Where however a trade union enters into a collective agreement, we find that disputes in relation to it are rarely, if ever, referred to the courts. This means that no formal sanction may exist in such circumstances, and if no formal sanction exists then, in a very direct way, we are confronted once again with Herbert Hart's distinction between a person being obliged, that is to say acting out of fear of some unpleasant consequence, and a person experiencing an obligation, that is to say experiencing the impact of rule-guidance. Where sanctions are weak or nonexistent, then the notion of rule-guidance becomes clearer and more open to exploration.

But why should sanctions be weak in such circumstances? This is a useful question in our exploration of the idea of obligation. In the first place there is the approach of the law to collective agreements. We find in the Trade Union Act 1871 that

nothing in this Act shall enable any court to entertain any legal proceedings instituted with the object of directly enforcing or recovering damages for the breach of .... (inter alia) any agreement made between one trade union and another.[17]

But this did not spring from any desire to place trade unions, in some sense, above the law but rather from a practical difficulty which was quite severe. Up to that time the law would do nothing to protect the property, contracts and trusts of trade unions on the general grounds that they possessed, among their principal purposes, objects which were in restraint of trade and therefore they were unlawful organisations. The act set out to remedy this by providing that

40

the purposes of any trade union shall not by reason merely that they are in restraint of trade, be unlawful so as to render void or voidable any agreement or trust.[18]

But this created a further problem, because now it might appear that the courts could be called upon to enforce an agreement between members concerning the conditions on which they should be employed, an agreement for the payment of subscriptions to trade unions and so forth. The act therefore went on to declare that while such agreements were lawful they would nevertheless be unenforceable in the courts, at least directly. And among the agreements which were seen by the act as being lawful but unenforceable were agreements between trade unions.

The reason therefore for such exemptions lay in certain difficulties concerning the very status of the trade union before the law. It follows that the legislators saw the provision as an unhappy one and provided for its very tight construction. For example, the act speaks of agreements between trade unions. Therefore, it does not cover a collective agreement between an employer standing alone and the trade union, although in Ireland it does cover a collective agreement between an employer's association and a trade union.

As far as the statute goes then, the area of nonjusticiability seems to be quite limited. The practice of the courts however, seems to be to extend this area of nonjusticiability. In an English case[19] the judge had regard principally to the intention of the parties, where the climate of opinion was generally against seeing collective agreements as legally binding and 'without clear and express provisions making them amenable to legal action they remained in the realms of undertakings binding only in honour. Neither party had the intention to make the agreements binding in law.' The position is somewhat less clear in Ireland. In Goulding's case[20] the Supreme Court, without much discussion on the topic, referred to such collective agreements as contracts, admittedly by way of *obiter*. When we set aside the special position under transport legislation, it is perhaps not entirely certain what the reference to contract was intended to imply, although some consider it as a clear enough indication that the courts would regard such collective agreements as binding in law.[21]

But the courts would tend to exclude such cases as well for another practical reason. The trade union in collective agreements is not an agent but a principal and cannot bind the members[22] even though the collective agreement is the context in which the member and his employer make their own perfectly binding contract. One could of course attempt to place a duty of enforcement on the trade unions in regard to their own members, as was attempted in the ill-fated 1971 Industrial Relations Act in the United Kingdom, and one might in addition ascribe to the contracting parties the defaults of non-contracting third persons, that is to say the members of the trade union. Such an approach however appears to be not only contrary to the general understanding of the common law in regard to vicarious responsibility but creates many practical difficulties of implementation. The second point we must make therefore is that in addition to certain statutory limitations on justiciability there are further practical reasons why the courts tend to exclude collective agreements from their area of concern.

The third point we must recognise is that the parties to collective agreements do not as a rule refer disputes arising from collective agreements to the courts of law. In the case of the employer this seems largely a question of expediency. When in Britain the 1971 Act raised the presumption of enforceability, Professor O. Kahn-Freund, usually the most judicious of men, thought that

unions may have to make concessions in order to induce management to consent to the (non-enforceability) clause.[23]

But in fact it never became a significant bargaining issue.[24] Employers readily agreed to the inclusion in collective agreements of the phrase 'this is not a legally enforceable agreement', thereby taking it out of the scope of the legislation, not least because if the employer were to proceed either against his own employees or their trade union in order to recover damages for breach of contract, he would be likely to protract considerably an industrial dispute which might well have been best forgotten.

The fact is then that there is in the practice of industrial relations a marked reluctance on the part of employers to avail of the law. Should we be tempted in these circumstances, despite the various reasons we have offered, to see in this, nonetheless, some pervasive weakness of will? Observers of considerable insight and knowledge have confessed some impatience. For example the very influential Donovan Commission remarked in its report:[25]

We are not in principle opposed to the use of legal sanctions for the enforcement of agreed procedures. No such sanctions can however be enforced without the active participation of the employer. There is no such thing as an 'automatic' sanction. It follows that sanctions will remain unworkable until a fundamental change in our system of industrial relations has led to a situation in which employers may be able and willing to use such rights as the law gives them. At the present time legislation making procedure agreements legally enforceable would not in fact be enforced and like all legislation that is not enforced would bring the law into disrepute.

Donovan here made the point in relation only to the enforcement of agreed procedures but it has a wider application. More than that it applies to the public authority (where indeed in many circumstances the remedy may actually lie) no less than to the employer. But quite apart from the self-interest of the employer which we have already recognised, there is a wider and more significant difficulty, one that inevitably influences the public authority as well. It is the reluctance of employer and public authority alike to invoke a law that could be shown to be ineffective, perhaps in a public and disorderly way (and this indeed would be regarded as a much greater peril to the repute of the law than its non-invocation).

And what of trade unions? The trade union distrust of the courts, as I have attempted to demonstrate elsewhere,[26] is not without cause. We can point to the thrust of the common law in these matters, the essential illegitimacy, as the law saw it, of any group organised to moderate free play in the disposition of labour, a reliance, as the courts developed it, on the doctrine of conspiracy in particular, a thrust so powerful that it was only partially contained by the very explicit provisions of the Trade Disputes Act 1906. We can point to the use of the injunction, a device derived from principles of equity, which in Ireland in any event seemed for a period to be availed of with unusual readiness to prohibit industrial action. And although these things can — in my view — be quite correctly explained away as having their origin in traditionalism rather than in prejudice against trade unions as such, nevertheless trade unions developed a considerable distaste for law courts and lawyers and opposed vigorously, for example, their involvement in the Irish Labour Court in 1946.[27]

We must emphasise however that we have spoken here of law courts and judges, not of the law. Indeed, since the great revolution in British parliamentary life in 1906, the trade unions have distinguished between statute law (as an achievement of parliamentary democracy) and judge-made law as they called it (the law as evolved in the courts) which they saw as class-ridden. It is reasonable to suggest in relation to statute law that trade unions not only do not always oppose but may indeed welcome certain statutory developments; as we shall see, this is very clear in the field of employment protection and as a means of inhibiting some forms of discrimination. It is when statute law appears to limit what they see as their traditional prerogatives that trade unions anxiously and indeed vehemently oppose it. But even this phenomenon does not occur in every trade union movement in every country, and in some sense may be peculiar to the United Kingdom, to Ireland and to such other countries where trade unions grew as it were from the grass-roots upwards not only unaided by statute but at times impeded by it. In countries such as New Zealand and Canada, and, as far as one can judge, in the majority of countries in Western Europe, where trade unionism developed within a statutory frame, trade unions are much more disposed to regard as legitimate the intervention of statute in their affairs, not excluding the sensitive area of the limitation of industrial action. We must recognise however that in Ireland and in Britain trade unions will tend to resist legal sanctions particularly in the area of collective bargaining. But this brings us to the very root of the discussion, the problem of acceptability or legitimacy in areas where, in practice, legal sanctions do not run.

The first point that requires emphasis once again is that none of this removes collective agreements from the area of right-doing and wrong-doing. A breach is still a breach. In industrial relations, no less than in any other human activity, we recognise the presence of *homo pius,* rule-guided man. Those who engage in industrial disputes are, in the ordinary business of living, as disposed to good order as any other citizen. One can at times be shaken by events and, although explanations can be found for many damaging acts, there is no doubt that some are inexcusable. Nevertheless, it is much more reasonable to assume in those engaged in industrial disputes a disposition of moral normality than it is to assume the contrary. We take it as axiomatic therefore that those engaged in industrial relations are as conscious of obligation as other citizens. More than that, where a trade union member is not engaged directly in an industrial dispute, he regards himself in large measure not as a trade unionist but as a citizen, and is as ready as anyone else to condemn the cruel consequences of certain forms of industrial action. Furthermore he, no less than other citizens, is well disposed to that general ordering of society which is expressed through law. When he himself is plunged into an industrial dispute, his circumstances are changed but his moral awareness is not.

We are not concerned then with the reality of obligation. This manifestly exists. We are concerned instead with the extent to which the obligations which are urged either on employers or on employees, acting in a collective sense, are seen by them to be legitimate.

4

In our earlier discussion on the problems associated with vicarious responsibility, we have noted a special problem in collective bargaining, the existence of two quite separate and distinct relationships, with quite substantially different characteristics. The first relationship is between the principals, the employer and the trade union representatives. When these two parties make a bargain the relationship is explicit and clear enough. The second relationship is between the representative and the collectivity he represents. For the purposes of the discussion it is more helpful to discuss the trade union in this context since the employer's position is much less complex.

If it were within the competence of the trade union official himself to discharge every aspect of the bargain, and if any departure from the bargain on his part could be attributed without question to his own default, then of course no great difficulty would arise. But the trade union representative is not in such a position. On the contrary he is acting for his members, not normally on an agency basis but on a representative basis. He cannot require in some quasi-contractual way that they honour the agreement that he has entered on their behalf. His task is to enter such agreements which in his best judgement, taking account of discussion, voting and other means of establishing support, are likely to be honoured in all particulars. This is the character of the second relationship, wholly different from the first since it consists not in a bargain between equal partners but in some rather sophisticated quasi-political understanding (something which Flanders of course was right in recognising). The legitimacy we discuss therefore must be explored not so much in the arena of the bargain but in the more political and complex arena of the trade union itself.

If one enters into a valid contract oneself, one's obligation is clear. Here, however, because the relationship is a vicarious one, legitimacy turns on the extent to which one feels one has been committed by the bargain, in circumstances where normally the law is either silent or obscure. Let us attempt to identify at least some circumstances where this problem is likely to occur.

We can see the problem clearly enough where the bargain is made at a level quite distant from the domestic employment. This occurs for example in the case of a centralised bargain and is a point which has always troubled the parties to the Irish national pay agreements. In 1964 there was, among the employers in any event, a very exacting sense in which the national agreement of that year bound the parties and if the trade unions were unable to ensure this exacting conformity on the part of their members, then in the employers' eyes they must be seen as inadequate either in their judgement or in their ability. The upshot was (although this was not the only reason) a collapse into a widespread series of different disputes, this being in fact the only national pay agreement to end in this way.[28] In the long series of national pay agreements which followed one upon the other during the 1970s, this difficulty was recognised by both sides. Provision was made for special adjustments in special cases during the course of the agreement and provision was also made for joint supervision and administration.[29] The trade unions on their part involved the grass-roots members more and more, many of the large unions balloting them individually in order to secure majority consent. Despite this, certain agreements, for example that in 1974 and again in 1978, had to be cast in somewhat flexible and permissive terms before consent could be secured.

One can see in the operation of these national pay agreements as well the problem of deterioration. That which appears legitimate at the outset can for a number of reasons lose its standing among trade union members and although one can provide to some degree for problems associated with the deterioration of money-values, it is difficult to anticipate the restlessness that grows from changing expectations. Deterioration must here be understood in the context of term agreements, that is to say agreements that automatically conclude once a stated term has expired but not until then. There was a time, in the 1940s and 1950s, when we had what are now described as open-ended national agreements, that is agreements which persisted until they were concluded or varied at the initiative of one or both of the parties. This was possible in those relatively stable days, but from the 1960s onwards term agreements became inevitable. The Labour Court[30] deplored the development, seeing it as contributing to higher expectations and higher anxieties, but the rapidity of economic and industral change required it. When we speak of deterioration within national pay agreements, therefore, we speak of the extent of the deterioration which will occur within the agreed term.

There can also be deterioration in a bargaining process. There is a very interesting example in the highly formalised systems of conciliation and arbitration, where the arbitrator confines himself to the material before him, largely being matters of pay comparabilities, and therefore insensitive to major changes within the grades being compared. In such circumstances one finds occasionally a recourse to review bodies, as in recent years in the case of the teachers and the police force where the purpose is (or should be) to realign groups in a manner which is seen to be more legitimate, although in practice it has led at times to an alternative and perhaps less legitimate form of arbitration.

This problem of deterioration is also evident in the manner in which domestic employment is managed. Productivity agreements, for example, are notoriously subject to deterioration since that which is intended to reward exceptional endeavour becomes, after a period, part of the expected income and consequently loses its original meaning. To some extent as well, all job evaluation schemes tend to deteriorate over time as both management and employees gain skill in their manipulation.[31]

But within the domestic situation there are many problems in effecting an adequate level of legitimacy among all. It is clear that the consent is slender when the majority who support the proposal is itself slender. It is clear as well that there are times when a majority vote is an inadequate if not an inequitable procedure. This occurs in particular where a bargain while benefiting a substantial majority bears harshly on a minority and even gravely disadvantages them. One finds in the reports of the appeals board of the Irish Congress of Trade Unions and on occasion in the reports of the disputes committee of the same organisation, quite a number of instances of this difficulty where members who see themselves disadvantaged in this way tend to break from their original union, seeking membership in another.[32]

If we consider convention and custom rather than the rules of collective agreements, we see them springing usually from the workers' side and creating at times a conflict with the provisions of the collective agreements often of an unexpected kind. This frequently occurs in the area of craft employment, where the union itself traditionally tends to regulate the employment no less than the employer. In the case of Guinness Brewery, James's Gate, for example, the craft unions traditionally took the view that

48

promotion to supervisory level was strictly a matter of seniority, that seniority operated strictly within each defined location in the Brewery and that a worker therefore who voluntarily moved from one location to another lost his seniority. The circumstances of ordinary living, illness perhaps, or the extent to which a movement was really voluntary, made the arrangement difficult to sustain, until eventually a new grade was formed by a reluctant management, a compensatory grade which gave the worker the wage of the supervisory grade without the responsibility and without the right to proceed further.

In the case of the Irish Bookbinders' and Allied Trades' Union, a number of men in a printing works refused to carry out a certain task. The management attempted to suspend them but a rule of the union obliged the men to refuse suspension, leaving the management with the alternative of dismissing them. The rule, the origin of which was obscure, was thought to have sprung from an early date when workers and their supervisor conspired to effect suspensions so that the men could attend race meetings, football matches or other significant events. The desire of the union to discipline their members had given rise to the rule and, although it was now meaningless it was still given, in the manner of the crafts, a great traditional significance.

These are merely examples of a state of affairs that is widespread, where not only is rule sometimes opposed to rule, convention to convention, but expectation is opposed to expectation, undermining in some degree the legitimacy of agreements. Nowhere is this more clear in Ireland than in public service employment, where for example if a grade, on the basis of increased productivity or of work reassessed (when compared to grades elsewhere), is rewarded with a salary increase, the increase is immediately followed by demands by others based not on grounds of performance but on grounds of strict relativity, on the restoration of a relationship in pay that previously existed.[33]

A trade union, committed to good order, will naturally seek such help as it can to overcome these difficulties, and it would appear at first sight that the more information it possesses about the attitude

49

of its members to such bargains the better. This leads us back in a very special way to the centre of our discussion.

Is there a contribution which the sociologist, and in particular those with skills in surveying attitudes, can make to all this? In the local and domestic disputes which I have described perhaps the arena is not quite large enough, but in the greater issues of national bargaining it would appear that there is certainly a place for such expertise. It should be possible to identify attitudes towards bargains with some degree of sophistication, and plot as well the manner in which these change over time. And yet in Ireland, neither in the area of national bargaining nor at the more domestic level, has any such survey been undertaken. This may reflect the inadequacy of social science in this country as yet. But neither has it been sought either by the employers or the trade unions. This I suspect springs from a belief that, while the procedure is interesting and helpful, it is essentially inadequate. The reason is that attitudes may not always be central to the idea of legitimacy. Indeed trade unions in practice find greater administrative security and equity in continuously emphasising to their members not feelings, not attitudes, but rationality and objectivity in the evaluation of bargains and in their subsequent support.

Perhaps we might explain the point in the following manner. In the early 1960s the Tavistock Institute of Human Relations was asked by the Norwegian government in the course of its examination of industrial democracy to survey the attitude of employees to worker-directors on company boards in those European countries where they then existed. It was found, among other things, that the existence of worker-directors did not appear to influence one way or the other the extent to which the workers had a favourable attitude to the company. It was apparently for this reason that the Norwegian government tended to emphasise in the years that followed the importance of participation at shop floor level. Nevertheless, towards the end of the 1960s a clear demand arose of an imperative kind for worker-directors established by statute and it has been suggested that this demand always existed but was not revealed by an attitude survey, the reason being that a political aspiration derives from some idea of a right which is seen to

50

exist independently of the manner in which one is treated by the society concerned, be it the political society of the state or the smaller society of the firm. Of course it might be urged that one could certainly devise a questionnaire of sufficient sophistication to meet this point, but I personally suspect that we must once again return to Herbert Hart and the notion of an observer within, not an observer without. Insofar as we rely on the information derived from an observer without, then we can take account only of those things which are causal in character, seeing disposition as the fount of action, but not judgement. Indeed, it must be assumed by the observer without that, for practical purposes, disposition determines judgement. Yet judgement, for good or ill, although frequently trapped by disposition is ultimately independent of it. The observer without, therefore, cannot identify that sense of right (so essentially a judgemental matter) which the employee experiences, that sense of obligation which he believes his employer owes him, which is, or can be, quite independent of the actual circumstances of the relationship between them.

This is in no way to discount the importance of survey work or indeed of industrial anthropology which could be remarkably helpful in the circumstances we have discussed, but such surveys must be seen in the light of these concepts of obligation and concepts of right, otherwise their results could be profoundly misleading.

5

We have then been prompted by Hart's concept of obligation and his image of a rule-guided society to undertake a form of analysis which can be fruitful in a number of practical ways. In particular, it provides us with criteria for evaluating institutions of the middle ground and, in the case of the Irish Labour Court, it provides us with some means of responding to the unease which the Court itself feels in regard to its own growing complexity of purpose,[34] an unease which we have already recognised but which we may now explore further. While the Court's primary function under the Industrial Relations Act

is to assist parties to settle their disputes, the national agreements in laying down standards and procedures to be observed by employers and workers for the resolution of problems which come within the scope of the Agreements have given the Court functions which were not envisaged for it under the Industrial Relations Act — functions of an interpretative nature in relation to certain provisions of the Agreements. ... New legislation has appreciably increased and made more complex the work of the Court by involving it in interpretative functions in arriving at determinations which have legal effect.

The difficulty here of course lies in the fact that the Court was established as a body whose purpose was to promote accommodation in disputes as to interest, to act as an honest broker, neither to apply law nor to create it. Therefore, as we have already recognised, it looked for no rule to apply, since no rule existed, and it eschewed precedent since it was wholly inappropriate, in its view, to create such rules. (To respect consistency is a somewhat different matter and is a much less demanding idea than the creation of binding precedents which is what rule-making requires.)[35] However, both in the area of national agreements and in the area of workers' statutory rights, the function given to the Court is to apply a rule, to administer a law of some kind, with all the discipline that this implies. An institution designed for one function cannot readily provide the other. The experience in the United Kingdom of the Advisory Conciliation and Arbitration Service and of the Northern Ireland Labour Relations Agency bears this out; such bodies are extraordinarily careful to avoid an adjudicatory role, even one remote from rule-enforcing such as arbitration. The Commission of Inquiry on Industrial Relations[36] recognised the same point in its recommendation on institutions, distinguishing between a Labour Relations Board and a Labour Relations Court, although as we have already remarked their insistence on regarding disputes between unions and recognition disputes as justiciable is puzzling and quite inconsistent with their own approach.

If, however, we look to the functions which need to be fulfilled by such institutions rather than at the various institutions with which we are familiar, then we can bring the analysis one step further and perhaps present it in a clearer fashion. The first function which the parties require of a third party institution, or an institution of the middle ground, is conciliation. The function here is to facilitate the making of a bargain or to provide a solution for a dispute of a non-bargaining kind. In the sense in which we use the term conciliation here, no third view is offered. The process is one of mutual clarification and a more exact method of communication since the conciliator (often moving from one party to another in separate rooms) may be able to communicate impressions and non-commital views which allow explorations of positions that would otherwise be impossible. The conciliator is a skilful instrument in the negotiation, not, in these circumstances, a determiner of the result. This is the most popular part of third party institutional service in industrial relations and is quite different as a function from one in which, in arbitration for example or in the case of a recommendation of the Irish Labour Court, an opinion is offered on how the problem might be remedied. This is seen as a distinct and different function and is of course organized separately in the Labour Court and in the Irish civil service conciliation and arbitration scheme, although both functions are contained within the same institutional framework. So great is the distinction however between this and conciliation that there are those who would urge very strongly, following the United Kingdom model, that the institutional arrangement should also be quite distinct. In neither case, it will be noted, are we dealing with rights; we are dealing merely with an accommodation of interests. And if in some arbitration procedures there is a considerable expectation that both parties will consent to the recommendation, this, as we have already seen, springs from some convention or other or perhaps an agreement to this effect in advance; it does not spring intrinsically from the nature of the function itself.

Next we come to the function of adjudication. Here again we are confronted with two quite different processes. In the first place we have the application of a rule which springs from a collective agreement. Such a rule is of course quite justiciable but as we have seen in the course of this discussion, sanctions for breach, for one reason or another, are rarely sought. There is, finally, the other area of justiciable matters, those rights, normally conferred by statute, familiar to the normal judicial process, and carrying sanctions in the ordinary way. Unfair dismissal and discrimination at work on grounds of sex are good examples of this and we shall discuss them, among others, in the next chapter.

It is clear however, that in regard to all these functions, with the exception of the last, the third party institution must rely essentially on its acceptability in the eyes of the parties concerned, its legitimacy, as we have described. There is not only the legitimacy of a rule, where a rule is appropriate, as for example in a collective bargain; we have seen now that there is also the question of the legitimacy of the institution that makes intervention. (This we shall discuss more fully when in ChapterIV we come to consider the public authority's role in creating such institutions.) It is not surprising then that considerable care has been taken from time to time to devise institutions which have this capacity. The Irish Labour Court is an example[37] where, unlike in a court of law, acceptability, not objectivity, was seen to be the principal characteristic of those appointed, even the chairman. While the Labour Court personnel are appointed for a reasonably extended period, there are other institutions, such as arbitration boards, where the chairman is appointed by agreement between the parties only for a reasonably brief period and the legitimacy of the appointment maintained largely by these means. A further example is the Employer Labour Conference under the national pay agreements of the 1970s. Here, certain adjudication functions were performed by a group headed by an independent chairman but heavily reliant on a small number of the top leaders of the trade unions and employers.

It follows from this that in all countries with advanced systems of industrial relations these functions will be sought by parties in dispute and although the institutions themselves that are created for the purpose may differ greatly in appearance and foundation the functions must necessarily remain the same. As we shall see in our concluding chapter this in turn can form a basis for comparison, a *tertium comparationis,* which would serve to promote international studies.

There is perhaps a final function which we have not covered, not as prominent as the others but nonetheless of great importance. This is the function of reform, always present but difficult to express in an institutional way. It usually consists in attempting to expand rule-guidance as far as it is appropriate to do so. As early as 1948 R.J.P.Mortished, recognising that disruptive action was much more likely to occur in the area of disputes as to interest, attempted to enshrine the industrial relations system in Ireland in a context of rule by means of a national agreement on pay and procedures,[38] and during the 1970s the national pay agreements were negotiated with the same object in view. In the wider market area, this deliberate promotion of rule is seen as well in the development in many countries of anti-trust, or restrictive practices, legislation. In Ireland, where the system is quite undeveloped, there are as yet no general prohibitions as, for example, of retail price maintenance or of restriction on entry, but the Restrictive Practices Commission, on a trade by trade basis, recommends within each particular trade or service, where this is appropriate, regulations peculiar to the circumstances of that trade and this is given the force of law. Much might be learned in industrial relations from such a procedure, as I have indicated elsewhere,[39] particularly where circumstances differ so much from employment to employment. It would be necessary, however, to approach the question of sanctions with some care.

In the next chapter we take up those obligations which spring not from agreements but from the rights which persons possess which are anterior to agreements, which are perhaps fundamental to the person or which in any event are guaranteed by statute.

CHAPTER THREE

Obligations arising from Personal Rights

1

Although we are concerned with industrial relations, it is necessary at the outset to consider, however briefly, the origin of personal rights in general so that we may set the scene for our specific discussion. Clearly personal rights can be created by lawmakers such as parliament, with no greater or more obvious authority than that of parliament itself. The right of workers to compensation in the event of injury, and the correlative obligation resting on the employers under the workmen's compensation legislation is a case in point. The obligation exists irrespective of the employer's culpability in the matter. Furthermore, as we shall see, there are in the conduct of business certain rules of the market, bearing largely on competitive practices, which for market reasons, and not for any reason more fundamental, confer rights on some traders in some circumstances and impose correlative obligations on others. The obligation to both equity and full disclosure in regard to terms of supply is a case in point. But these rights and the obligations they impose are constructed to meet special needs and derive their legitimacy not from any obvious natural or fundamental right of a personal kind but from their appropriateness and from the authority of the body that created them. But appropriateness and authority are the very things which from time to time come under question in industrial relations. Consequently, in this brief discussion we shall begin by considering fundamental rights, rights which exist in the person in some antecedent way, that is to say antecedent to positive law, rights which, as Hart points out,[1] the law recognises rather than creates. If such a fundamental right is seen to exist, the expectation is that it will legitimate the correlative obligation in a manner which raises it above disputes concerning institutional authority.

But here we are presented with a difficulty. Such rights, if they are to be effective, must have clear expression. In our search for some recitation of such fundamental rights, there is much that is uncertain. We may find their expression rooted in the continuous decisions of the courts rather than explicitly set out in statute. We may find that even where a statute does confirm the right it may do so in a limited way, leaving much to be developed later.

One might be tempted to suggest that in a country such as Ireland, which has a written constitution, our search for anterior rights need not be a difficult one. In particular, articles 40 to 44, declaring themselves to be concerned with fundamental rights, are intended to meet just this point. But the difficulty is still there. The Supreme Court in recent times has developed a doctrine of unspecified constitutional rights, deriving them by way of interpretation from 'other clauses in the Constitution or from the Christian and democratic character of the State.'[2]. Once one advances the idea of an unspecified constitutional right one raises the need to specify it, a duty which the courts see themselves as fulfilling. We therefore must conclude that as the law stands there is some corpus of personal rights, anterior to positive law, which must be recognised by the courts and applied by them but which, although in substantial measure contained in basic legal documents such as constitutions and also in statute, is by no means exhausted by such instruments.

But if the courts rely on such a concept of their role, it raises at times the suspicion that they are making law rather than administering it, that they do not, as they claim, merely recognise some clear, antecedent if unspecified, right and apply it, but are actually in the business of creating such rights by the weight of their decisions. This however may not be so. Let us contrast two cases in order to clarify the matter. The point of law in these cases is not significant here; what is significant is the extent to which the court believes itself to be relying on anterior law. Lord Devlin in the well-known case of *Nagle v. Feilden*[3] remarked:

58

The true ground of jurisdiction in all these cases is a man's right to work. I have said it before and I repeat it now, that a man's right to work is just as important to him as, perhaps more important than, his rights of property. Just as the courts will intervene to protect his rights of property, they will also intervene to protect his right to work.

The fact that the right to work is a difficult concept and juridically undefined in no way lessened Lord Devlin's sense of conviction that he was dealing with an important anterior right. But one finds no such air of convinced righteousness in the difficult Irish case of *Talbot (Ireland) Ltd. v. Merrigan and Others*[4] where the court, in a haphazard, unreported and remarkably casual manner appeared, in a case concerning an injunction to restrain picketing, to offer views on the merits of the case at the interlocutory stage. At such a stage in the proceedings it is not unusual for the courts to rely, not on some view of the merits, but rather on the idea of a balance of convenience until such time as the matter comes to trial, but in an industrial dispute the concept of balance of convenience is a very uncertain one.[5] Yet if other reasons are adduced for a decision, they must, because the proceedings are interlocutory, be provisional in character. In Talbot's case it seems to me the court was obliged to proceed to judgement on an uncertain base neither with a clear rule to guide it nor with the support of some traditional and committed view of what was right as was so manifestly the case in *Nagle v. Feilden*. This then was the reason for the unsatisfactory result. If a judgement is to be made securely it must be based on the notion of some external criterion or principle, even if it is merely a convention, or a tradition, or something as impalpable as the judge's own abiding sense of justice. It cannot be a matter of subjective preference which the notion of a balance of convenience or a hasty assessment of the merits in some measure implies.

But these are dangerous and unsettling ideas in the field of industrial relations since there are many who would say that the judges, coming as they do from a group of some privilege, would carry their prejudices with them into industrial disputes calling to their aid not some anterior sense of right-doing but some anterior expectation of the way society should be organised. Sir William Erle, a doughty champion of individualism in these matters, saw this danger being offset, if not entirely discounted, by the very quality of a judge's prudence, a quality recognised by his contemporaries and validated by his successors.[6] But this again might be regarded as merely a confirmation of the prejudices of a particular group in society and that further validation is necessary.

And so it is urged that despite difficulty and uncertainty in its identification there is indeed some antecedent understanding of what is right, antecedent to statute, antecedent to constitutional expression and antecedent to the formulations of the common law, and that this is the ground on which positive law rests. I find myself not only compelled to such a view but compelled as well to recognise in it something of the great tradition of natural law. But this is an area of debate which we need not enter. Even where I recognise the true existence of some anterior system of rights and obligations which we may describe as natural law and which positive law must in some sense acknowledge, I must recognise as well that positive law and natural law are not necessarily in direct correlation. Between them there lies what one might describe as consensual law. This consensual law is the traditional notion of justice which a society possesses, usually determined over time and therefore prescinding from occasional lapses into national wrong-doing. It is related to natural law in that it attempts to express a general awareness of what is right, and yet there is no reason to believe that it corresponds directly to it.

I am not in this urging any superiority for what I have described as consensual law. No matter how respected as a procedure, a head count on a moral issue must surely be irrelevant, whether we describe the result as a majority or as a consensus, and further I am troubled but unconvinced by notions of the general will and its various expressions. The ground of right must lie beyond all this. The fact remains, however, that for our purposes in industrial relations, and indeed for much political activity, it is this consensus that validates, empirically at least, the operation of a rule, however defective or inadequate that consensus may be.

Consensual law then, while it may reflect natural law and while it may correspond to it in considerable measure, nonetheless finds its grounding in the notion of the consensus, that is a commitment to such rights and duties as spring sensibly and pragmatically from an assembly of those ideas that are considered appropriate. Natural law is not in practice its ground of legitimacy; the assembled interests of the citizens as a whole appear to be. This is why states may go to war, or commit great injustices against minorities and yet by consensus remain legitimate. If therefore the fundamental law rests on a consensus we are confronted with a troublesome uncertainty. Since a consensus by its nature is not absolute but provisional then we are in our Western societies, even those of us profoundly committed to the idea of absolutism as a ground of law, nevertheless committed in practice to the notion of provisional rights. This is the empirical base from which we must construct our understanding of personal rights as they apply in the field of industrial relations.

There is uncertainty therefore both in regard to the basis for a right (because the notion of a consensus is itself a difficult one) and in regard to its expression. Yet we must make some attempt to delineate what certain rights mean if we are to explore the difficult and conflictual set of norms which underlie industrial relations. We regard as central to the discussion not so much enactments but rather the manner in which the rights and obligations emerged through the courts, since here we find reflected first the give and take of disputation. We can then go on and see, in a more graphic way, the formulation of these rights in Constitution and in statute.

There is finally a technical distinction which we must make. Where the state intervenes to establish positive law, whether fundamental or statutory, it does so for one of two reasons, either to confirm or create personal rights primarily in the interests of the citizen (as articles 40 to 44 of the Constitution do, or as the employment protection acts do) or, on the other hand, primarily to defend or promote the public interest, as much trade union regulatory legislation does. These two categories are by no means secure and exclusive, but the identification of the primary motive is important. When the state acts in what it conceives as the public interest it may well be seen as a third party in a tangled dispute rather than the harbinger of consensus, while such a peril is unlikely to arise where the purpose is essentially the formulation of

61

a personal right of citizenship. In this part of the discussion we are concerned only with such personal rights of citizenship, and we leave the other topic to the next chapter.

2

If, in political matters, the consensus can be at times uncertain in its support of fundamental law and therefore not only provisional in character but at times troubled by inherent contradictions, the consensus is much more uncertain in the field of industrial relations. Frequently the rights that arise in employment are discovered in the context of an industrial dispute, and while this is by no means always the case, nevertheless it is the area of central importance to us in this study. In such circumstances of industrial dispute, the validation of rights by means of consensus is inevitably beset with difficulties. The moral construct of a dispute will frequently look quite different depending on one's viewpoint; indeed one may find each party not so much answering the ethical question in a different manner but differing as to the question itself. Let me offer an example in an introductory way to help clarify the issue. Certain members of a trade union, employed by the Educational Company of Ireland Ltd.,[7] attempted to bring pressure to bear on nine of their colleagues who were non-members to join the union and when their efforts were unavailing they

then sought to bring pressure to bear on them by endeavouring to force (the Company) to compel them to join the union or to dismiss them if they did not do so. This the plaintiffs refused to do and the defendants went on strike and picketed the plaintiffs' premises.

The Supreme Court held that the provisions of the Trade Disputes Act 'authorising a trade dispute to coerce persons to join a union against their will' are void as being repugnant to the provisions of the Constitution. This at first sight seems a straightforward case. Certain citizens had established that a union was engaging in coercing them to become members on pain of dismissal from their employment, and the question they asked of the Court was a question which related to their right not to be interfered with in the exercise of a fundamental freedom. However, if one were to look at the matter from the point of view of the trade union members one would find that they, in some distress concerning their conditions of work, had only recently joined the union, an act which they understood their employers greatly deplored. As they saw it if their nine colleagues did not join the union as well, their own position within the firm would be greatly imperilled. The question to them was a question of mutual defence against a hostile employer, and the answer of the court, which turned on the right of a citizen to be free in the matter of association, appeared to them to be intrinsically irrelevant.

On the other hand, despite the deep conflict of view in such disputes the commitment of each party to the idea of obligation and right is in no way diminished and to this important point we shall have occasion to return.

We must therefore approach the problem once again from the position of each actor, not adjudicating on such a position as much as exploring each party's understanding of it. We take first the employer, examining the nature of his freedom and the manner in which he is confronted with the obligations he owes his employees. The rights which these employees possess, which give rise to his obligation, may be seen as individual rights merely, or may be seen as giving rise to the rights of a collectivity. Secondly we take the freedom of employees, and in particular employees in a collectivity, to pursue their interests, a freedom which is also limited, limited by the obligation they owe to their employer (and at times to the public as a whole) and also by the obligation they owe to other workers.

3

What then of the employer? We take first his freedom to seek his own interest where he may. That he should have such a freedom is a powerful tradition in our society and it is often associated in some profound way with ideas of personal autonomy. In the nineteenth century, in the developing circumstances of a strongly competitive Britain in world markets, it was seen to be the trader's charter, which not only guaranteed him the opportunity of prosperity, but guaranteed the nation prosperity as well. Its unreasonable constraint therefore was not only an unwarranted interference with the trader[8] but a public wrong in that it did damage to the very engine of progress. Trading freely implied an absence of constraint, except where such constraints were reasonable and necessary, and certainly there could be no dispute about such constraints if they were freely accepted by the trader by way of contract. Let us consider first the employer in his relationship with the individual employee, taking up in a moment his relationship with the employees' collectivity.

Where therefore an individual employee had a contract, he could rely on it, but the very freedom of the market, and the vigour which attended this idea, meant that he could rely — by right — on little else. A world ruled by voluntary contract was a world of freedom to pursue self-interest in a righteous manner without the deadwood of traditional obligation. Sir Henry Maine, whose influence on nineteenth century thinking in these matters was so considerable, saw the movement towards contract at that time —and the growing dominance of contract over status — as the characteristic of progressive societies.[9] If, in accordance with such thinking, the relationship between employer and employee were essentially a contractual one, then once the terms of the contract were observed, no other obligation could arise — certainly no obligation enforceable at law. If the contract permitted the employer to terminate the employment on one week's notice — or on one day's notice — then this was the extent of his obligation, and circumscribed any remedies which the employee might seek.

The harshness of much of the conditions of factory work — only reluctantly ameliorated by statute — gave way in the early years of the present century to forms of work reorganisation which reduced a worker's contribution, in many large undertakings, to mechanical fragments, making him as replaceable in the process as any mechanical unit. All this inhibited in large measure that context of social obligation which even quite an elementary community of traders possesses, giving the employer yet greater freedom from constraint in the manner in which he pursued his interest. I do not

64

suggest of course that this was a society without concern or compassion, but such things formed no ground of right. The sense of righteousness that lay often with such trading took little account of those who held another view, those who claimed that all who participated in the community of work were possessed of some rights of a fundamental kind which were anterior to any found in a contract of employment.

However, since the last war, there has been a remarkable change in the attitude of society — particularly in western Europe — in relation to all this. It has been summarised in the concept of the individual's right to work. This must be distinguished as an idea from the political ideal of work for all — or full employment —which while a dominant guide in governmental policy is not of course actionable in the hands of the unemployed man or woman. What is actionable, what becomes the basis of the obligation, is the right of the worker to be continued in the employment unless it can be demonstrated that this right is overborne either by malfeasance on his part or by external circumstances, a right which in the view of some could be extended as well to just and favourable conditions of employment. Dr Franz Mestitz of the University of Frankfurt has observed:[10]

The recognition of these rights however means that questions of the continuance of the employment relationship and the regulation of its contents can in principle to a large extent no longer be answered by reference merely to individual contracts but must be looked at largely in the context of a supracontractual system. And here we can see a further fundamental development occurring in modern labour law. Protection of the individual by a right to work reveals a development recognised by Karl Renner as a movement from the idea of employment as something inherently changeable and uncertain, and dependent upon the economic forces operating in the particular situation, to the notion of a more or less permanent position, to a large extent unaffected by economic forces, and giving the worker a right in respect of his job rather like the trader's goodwill in his business. One can see in this a 'feudalisation' of the employment relationsip and an inversion or reversal of the movement from status to contract which Sir Henry Maine propounded as a general principle of legal development.

At the outset of this chapter we laid much stress on the fact that we must in the nature of things expect normative conflict, that this is the practical reality, the existence of strong differences in what men understand to be right. Yet in this area we find no such conflict at least in regard to principle. The enactments both in the United Kingdom and in Ireland which gave legal ground to such rights were widely accepted.[11] One would not anticipate that the trade unions would find in them much difficulty; this was a form of legislation which traditionally they not only accepted but actively sought. But what of employers? Let us look at the United Kingdom where the development of these ideas is quite well documented. At first sight the employer response appeared to be merely a practical one, a matter almost of necessity. It was a time of economic growth with a strong promise of its continuance; trade unions were tough-minded and could be expected to pursue job security by industrial action if this were required and in any event the climate of opinion throughout Europe appeared to be in favour of such developments. Indeed Fair Deal at Work which could be expected to represent in good measure the conservative employer's view remarked that Britain was one of the few countries where dismissals were a frequent cause of strike action and went on:[12]

It seems reasonable to link this with the fact that Britain is one of only seven out of the sixty-two countries covered in an ILO study of the subject where dismissal procedures are not regulated by statute.

But the significant thing is that there was more in this opinion than merely pragmatism and expediency. Fair Deal at Work urged a change in law and practice 'both on the grounds of principle and as a means of removing a major cause of industrial disputes'.

This was so, even though some of the provisions of the enactments were quite onerous, the Irish provisions tending to follow quite closely those in the United Kingdom.[13] That there should be a full judicial apparatus was to be expected, as were certain absolute prohibitions, such as dismissal by reason of sex, race, religion or membership of a trade union. But the most dramatic, and from the employer's point of view potentially the most onerous, was that the onus of proof in regard to the validity of the dismissal was shifted to the employer. It was this that gave rise to suggestions that in some sense a worker had a property in his

66

job[14] of which he could not, without good reason or without compensation, be deprived, since to say to an employer that he had no discretionary right within his contract to dismiss implied no less. It was this provision that was later modified to some degree by the Employment Act 1980;[15] but the thrust of the legislation remained. It remained despite the collapse of confidence in growth and the dismal and formidable decline in employment. Irish employers, too, while confessing anxiety by reason of these constraints have not challenged the principles of the legislation which still rest on the firm consensus as before. Of course there are occasional splurges of industrial action centering on dismissals, but these have usually some wider industrial import; disputes on dismissals *per se* do not as a rule lead to industrial action. While in early years, therefore, the relationship between an employer and an individual employee was often harsh and inequitable, there has, as we have seen, developed a consensus as expressed by recent legislation, and this on the whole has been free of that normative conflict, that consensual disarray, which we anticipated at the beginning of this chapter.

But if we look at the rights not of a worker but of a collectivity of workers, we find ourselves in an area of considerable difficulty. In the next section we shall consider a collectivity of workers in the active sense as exercising its own particular freedoms, so that we may explore the obligations which it owes to others. Here however, we are concerned with the collectivity as a possessor of rights which, in imposing obligations on an employer, limits his discretion in the pursuit of his interests. When we discussed earlier the distinction between a freedom and a right, we were careful to point out that a freedom has no correlative obligation. It could be urged that a collectivity has significance only in the sense that it is proactive, that is to say, exercising a freedom, and therefore no question of right arises in respect of which there might be an obligation. But on the contrary it could also be urged that a collectivity possesses a right to exist and a right furthermore to such things which, if they were constrained, would render its existence nugatory. This is why we find trade unions claiming from an employer what is described as recognition and responsible collective bargaining. Where this is denied by the employer,

67

industrial difficulties frequently follow. Although such a right is passionately urged by trade unions, it has apparently little standing in the traditions of the common law as we shall see in a moment. Statute law however has frequently attempted to provide worker collectivities with a secure legal base, not only in regard to affirming their right to exist, but in going further and attempting to ensure as well both recognition by the employer and also the opportunity for realistic collective bargaining. The most recent example was the Employment Protection Act 1975 and in particular section 11 (and the consequential sections) which have now been repealed. When however the public authority moves in this way it is more concerned with the promotion of the public interest rather than with the promotion of trade union rights and the discussion on the matter is therefore appropriate to Chapter IV. In general it can be said that the sense of righteousness which a trade union member may possess when he urges the right of his trade union to exist and to bargain is not as a rule reflected by the employer, indeed quite the contrary, although in practice and for reasons of practical common sense he will normally respond very rapidly to the request for collective bargaining.

4

What then of a collectivity of workers, and the constraints on its freedom by reason of its obligation to others? We set this discussion in the context of dispute since this is the major preoccupation of this study.

So conflictual is this whole field that it is important to remind ourselves that a basic consensus nevertheless does exist, that differences of view in relation to what obligations are appropriate are not radical, that is to say are not wholly mutually exclusive. In a word, as we have already emphasised, while the area is something of a jungle, it is a jungle inhabited by moral men who, on the whole, seek a resolution of their conflicts in a reasonable manner. True, it is made much more difficult in that there is an assumption that in matters of right and wrong, unlike in matters of mere interest, there can be only one correct view and it must prevail. But this in a way constitutes the imperative to find the consensus, building out as it were from a common commitment to good order. Before we begin to discuss the different understandings of obligation therefore we should once again emphasise that although we are in an area of deeply held convictions, not as to interest but as to right, often in opposition one to another, we are also in an area where there is by and large a fundamental commitment to good order. We have made this point already and one recognises that it might be challenged as to fact; one might point to instances of gross self-interest, bloodymindedness and indifference to the public welfare. Of course, such perversity exists but in general it can be contained. This at first sight may appear surprising, and perhaps, before we continue, we might offer a word of explanation. Let us begin by considering one or two examples. In the early seventies the Irish Bank Officials Association, a particularly militant organisation, engaged in a number of disputes with their employers in the course of which they rejected nationally agreed pay norms which had been negotiated generally by the employers and the trade unions. The government in these circumstances introduced legislation specifically limiting increases in pay which could be conceded by the banks. The dispute therefore was a three-cornered one reaching a serious crisis in August of 1976.[16] A final proposal was made to the union which fell far short of the very minimum which they regarded as being satisfactory. The executive committee, confident that it would be rejected, issued the proposal for ballot with a strong recommendation for rejection. In fact the proposal was accepted, albeit by a small majority. It is interesting to note, in regard to this case, that the Irish Bank Officials' Association appeared to be in conflict with the disciplines which had been accepted by the trade union movement as a whole and further that their industrial action was regarded with a good deal of hostility by the community in general.

A more dramatic example was the strike of the Shift-Workers Association in the Electricity Supply Board in April 1972. These were an entirely unofficial group, quite small in number, but capable, by reason of their special position, of bringing the whole electricity network to a standstill. Their action was seen by all, including other employees of the Board, as being remarkably cynical and self-interested. The strike, when it did occur on 12 April, was initially both effective and dangerous. The Irish Congress of Trade Unions issued a statement calling on all workers in the employment of the Electricity Supply Board to 'co-operate in securing that the maximum possible amount of electricity is made available, and full output resumed as soon as possible.' This meant that the trade unions advised their members to pass the shift-workers' pickets. But this was not enough. If the unique work of the shift-workers were not done, then power could not be restored. It was one thing to pass a picket; it was quite another to do the work of striking members. In trade union tradition it is normally regarded as unforgiveable. It was in these circumstances that the Irish Congress of Trade Unions, supported by the Draughtsman's and Allied Technicians' Association, instructed their engineering members to take over the shift-workers' duties and urged that, far from being hindered, they should be supported in this by members of the other unions. This in fact was done and although there was confusion for some time the strike collapsed.[17]

Even what appears to be the most perverse of all recent Irish disputes, the maintenance craftsmen's dispute of 1969[18] actually reinforces the point of good order. This was a very powerful group, apparently grossly disorganised, but sustained by a nucleus of engineering workers acting substantially in an unofficial way but with enormous determination and ruthlessness, causing prolonged and extensive damage not only to Irish industry but to many thousands of other workers. At first sight it could be said that the strike was successful in that the employers capitulated and it was a capitulation and not a settlement that brought the strike to an end. Nevertheless, the magnitude of the disaster and the sense of outrage which was generally felt among employers and trade unions alike contributed substantially to the idea of reform and led, in some part at least, to the series of national pay agreements which gave such stability to pay-bargaining during the decade of the seventies.

Let us suggest an explanation. In the first place it seems clear that where a dispute is actively resented by the public, not merely tolerated in a negative way, then the likelihood of its continuance is small. This is so even where, in terms of economic and organisational power, the collectivity is apparently in a very dominant position. The reason may lie in the view of the trade union of its own dispute activity. This is an area where we are helped in particular by the greater sophistication of Hart's analysis. If one saw an industrial dispute as simply a power conflict one would take little account of the sense of righteousness, or lack of it, on the part of the workers themselves. Yet it is central. It is not so much that it sustains the workers in dispute; what is much more significant is that in the nature of things it tends to reflect in some degree the view of the community as a whole, and consequently tends to be undermined if the community is very hostile. This is not surprising. Trade union members are not a tribe apart, and where a trade union member, as we already have had occasion to remark, is not engaged directly in an industrial dispute he regards himself in large measure not as a trade unionist but as a citizen. It seems odd to offer as an example of this the events which surrounded the collapse of the 1971 Industrial Relations Act in the United Kingdom. But it does demonstrate the point in a number of ways. Even though the Conservative government anticipated that the act would give rise to considerable hostility they nevertheless relied on this sense of orderliness and propriety on the part of all, including trade union members, to see them through, and indeed were it not for the miners' strike it is likely enough that the trade union movement as a whole would not have brought its protest further than the negative business of non-cooperation. We can see in the case of this ill-fated experiment in statute law that there was a great reluctance on the part of trade unions to enter into direct challenge in such circumstances and indeed the impetus to confrontation on the issue of law was as much if not more the responsibility of the Heath government as it was of the trade unions. As Brian Weekes and his colleagues in their commentary on the act remarked:[19]

Perhaps the greatest presumption of all was that respect for the law, and a belief in the 'rule of law' would ensure the act's operation and success, and that such a respect for the law would override other considerations if the

71

interests of any party to a dispute appeared to be threatened by the intervention of the courts.

Although the act collapsed somewhat ignominiously, the point about the general disposition of society towards good order should not be underestimated.

In industrial disputes then, a sense of right-doing is of considerable importance and further, when a dispute is such as to involve the public at large, then this right-doing must be something which the public in some sense recognises as well even though in a negative way. One cannot deny that there will be perverse disputes which will succeed but on the whole the moderation of right-doing is a powerful one. A workers' collectivity therefore in pursuing its freedoms will be sensitive to its obligations and this is the assumption on which we base the analysis which follows.

When a collectivity of workers, being in dispute with an employer, engages in industrial action, there are three areas in which the obligations it owes to others may constrain it. The first is the general obligation to the public interest, and this we shall take up in the course of the next chapter. The second is the obligation to the employer and the third is the obligation to other workers who may be adversely affected. We shall take the last first, since it permits us to continue our discussion on the right to work as possessed by the individual worker, but now seen from a different perspective. It must now be seen as a source of obligation which constrains a workers' collectivity in its freedom to act.

Let us then consider the freedoms of the collectivity and how they are grounded, approaching the question first in a general way and then more specifically considering the individual worker and how he might be affected by the exercise of these freedoms. The notion of trade union freedoms tends to be viewed differently by the different groups that encounter them, as we have already remarked, and we take each of these views in turn, first that of the public authority (concerned with the promotion of private rather than public interest), secondly the trade union view of itself, thirdly, in so far as this might briefly be indicated, the employer view and finally the view of the courts deriving from their own traditions.

Since trade unions were seen under the common law as unlawful organisations, and therefore at all times vulnerable, the concern of the public authority in its enactments both in the United Kingdom and in Ireland was to give trade union activity some status. Initially, in 1871,[20] an attempt was made to domesticate trade unions as such within the law but this had the unexpected effect of making the trade unions themselves and such assets as they possessed more rather than less vulnerable.[21] It was in these circumstances that the Trade Disputes Act 1906 abandoned the attempt to give status to a trade union as such (apart from protecting its assets under section 4), concentrating instead on the conferring of certain immunities in relation to its activities, that is to say in relation to peaceful picketing and in relation to interfering with another's business. (These are matters which we shall take up more specifically when we come to consider the arena of an employer's rights.) But the consequence of this was that the notion of a trade union as such became shadowy, since any passing group of workers, coming together for a particular purpose, constituted in some sense a trade union. But this obviously was going too far. A public authority in these circumstances could be expected to wish to confine such immunities, which after all are exceptional in our society, to established and responsible bodies and this they have continuously attempted to do by way of statute, the Irish example being the Trade Union Act 1941.

There were of course elements in the 1941 Act which went well beyond this and which set out indeed to reconstruct the Irish trade union movement. These were vigorously opposed by the trade unions and this is understandable. What is interesting however is that even where the statutory provision does no more than reinforce a current trade union practice it is looked on askance by the trade unions. This perhaps could be explained in part by the difficulty in distinguishing, in any statute, between the mere reinforcement of a trade union practice and the imposition of a regulation in the wider public interest. But it appears that there is more to it than that. Some evidence for this can be gained from the consent which trade unions generally, and specifically the Irish trade union movement, have given to Convention 87 of the

International Labour Organisation[22] which very strongly reinforces the idea of excluding the public authority from intervening in trade union affairs by means of regulation whatever the motive for that regulation might be. This convention has been quoted with approval by the Irish Congress of Trade Unions on more than one occasion.

It is this that leads to a consideration of the trade union movement's view of itself and of its freedoms. For this purpose let us continue the discussion on the nature of a collectivity, but seeing it now from a trade union point of view. It is obvious that the trade union movement could not in any sense approve of a fragmentary and disparate type of organisation. Indeed, on the whole, it seeks stability and cohesiveness. It deplores the multiplicity of bargaining units which fragmentation implies. On the other hand there is the profound conviction within the trade union movement that such structural or operational changes must be effected by the trade union movement itself. There is a deeply-felt although not very explicit view that a democratic association must in some sense provide in an ultimate way for the resolution of internal disputes; if this were not the case, if there were recourse to some body outside the democratic society, then its democratic character would somehow be impaired.

This raises more questions than are implied by the democratic principle alone and invites a wider consideration of what trade union freedoms might be. There is a certain view within the trade union movement which would see that movement as in some sense an imperium in imperio — a matter which Arnold Toynbee remarked on.[23] Here not only the trade union movement as a whole but each union, would be regarded, at least in some degree, as sovereign. Let us take a quite domestic example. Trade unions are very sensitive when it comes to the idea of an appeal by a member against decisions or actions of the trade union itself. The Irish Congress of Trade Unions, after a great deal of heart-searching, established an appeals board for such a purpose in 1964,[24] and it is only in recent times that the TUC in Britain agreed to the establishment of a TUC Appeals Committee of three,[25] but the ideal from a trade union point of view would be to regard the union

74

itself as the appropriate body to provide the final court of appeal for all internal matters. But this is merely a symptom. The disposition we seek to describe is to some degree a consequence of economic conflict, to some degree a question of tradition. When men for example are engaged in a major dispute where their sense of righteousness is strong, they tend to regard what their trade union stands for and their responsibility to it as being more significant than the broader responsibilities of citizenship; they tend to see their trade union not so much as a lesser society within a larger comity, but in some sense as an alternative, if not a sovereign, democracy, at least in a limited way. Of course, this may be explained in large part as the result merely of some equity denied, or even strident self-interest in borrowed clothes, but there are occasions where one can see as well the influence of certain trade union traditions. The socialist tradition of the international working class and its solidarity, while not promoting international co-operation to any degree, nonetheless may be seen as transcending national norms of conduct in the interests of a greater working class society, weakening as a result the notion of the state, and its legislative and judicial arms, as the ultimate authority. There is a further tradition of viewing a government as a stakeholder with special objectives which may be influenced by considerations of privilege and its defense. One would not wish to exaggerate this last aspect of things and in any event we shall investigate it further in the next chapter.

It is impossible, in the case of the employers, to offer a single coherent view, but it does appear broadly speaking that they will tend, in this area as in collective bargaining, to do those things which appear to them to be expedient and while in some cases the advent of a trade union may be seen as the disruptive expression of a minority view by a small number of employees, its existence frequently is regarded as a source of stability and responsible negotiation. We are unlikely to find among employers generally therefore any great desire to hold to the idea of the fundamental unlawfulness, or perhaps inappropriateness, of trade union organisation.

The position is quite other however when we come to the great

75

tradition of common law. The common law sees fundamental rights as being appropriate to a natural person and not to collectivities. Consequently if a conflict arises between an individual citizen and a trade union it is the fundamental rights of the citizen that become significant rather than those of the collectivity.

It might be urged in oppposition to this that the Irish Constitution does in fact give a substantial basis for the existence of trade unions and for their legitimate activities. It seems to me that this is not the case; rather does the Constitution offer an opportunity for a more explicit development of the common law position. Under the Irish Constitution

the State guarantees liberty for the exercise of the following rights, subject to public order and morality ... the right of the citizens to form associations and unions. Laws, however, may be enacted for the regulation and control in the public interest of the exercise of the foregoing right. Laws regulating the manner in which the right of forming associations and unions and the right of free assembly may be exercised shall contain no political, religious or class discrmination.

There are two words in this passage, which although used together here, are carefully distinguished one from another in the context of the analysis which we have used so far in this study. The two words are, liberty, on the one hand and, right, on the other. It seems to me however that in the constitutional passage, one can properly discard the word liberty since the same passage could be expressed negatively, that is to say, the state guarantees that a citizen shall not be interfered with in the exercise of his right to form associations and unions, except where the interference is in accordance with law. In doing this however, we have converted the plural of the Constitution (the right of the citizens) into a singular (the right of the citizen).

One could conclude from this that the plural in the Constitution must be understood in a distributive sense, not in a collective sense. We find this borne out in the leading cases on the question, in particular the Educational Company of Ireland Ltd. v. Fitzpatrick[26] from which flowed the doctrine, which seems now reasonably well established, that the right to associate carries with it the right not to

76

be coerced into association. If we were to recast both propositions negatively their close relationship becomes clear enough. A citizen has a right not to be interfered with in forming a union and he has a right not to be interfered with if he chooses not to be associated with a union formed by others.

We cannot find then in all this any necessary guarantees to the collectivity as such (though they may exist). What we find prominently is a guarantee to a citizen in relation to a collectivity. The common law of England, more traditionally and more unambiguously, declares the same thing. It does not see a collectively and its rights; it sees only the individual. This then is the very heart of the normative conflict.

The arena within which this conflict is worked out is more often than not the closed shop. The closed shop ultimately turns on the non-employment or disemployment of individual workers. If they are to work they must be members of a trade union. In this way the trade union interest and the individual interest are opposed.

Normally speaking closed shops are of two kinds, what is known as the pre-entry closed shop (that is to say a situation in which a condition for application for employment is the prior membership of a trade union) and a post-entry closed shop (that is to say a situation in which a condition of the employment contract itself is that the employee join the appropriate union on his being appointed). We consider the pre-entry closed shop first.

The pre-entry closed shop has been treated very roughly by the courts. On the whole they see in it a licence to work exercised by an organisation which has no such entitlement. If a person, possessing a certain skill, is not a member of the union which represents that skill, then that union will do all it can to ensure that he does not work. Furthermore if he happens to be expelled from the union, he is expelled from the exercise of his skill. The central issue therefore is the right to work, in the sense of the right to earn one's living, and the obligation which such a right imposes on a trade union in promoting its own interests.

Salmon, L.J. in *Nagle's* case, to which we have already referred, has said[27]

I should be sorry to think that ... we have grown so supine that today the courts are powerless to protect a man against an unreasonable restraint upon his right to work to which he has in no way agreed but which a group with no authority, save that which it has conferred on itself, seeks capriciously to impose upon him. I certainly refuse to believe that it is not even arguable that in such circumstances the courts have power to protect the individual citizen.

And in 1971 Lord Sachs in his judgement in the case of *Edwards v. S.O.G.A.T.*[28] reinforced the point:

A rule that in these days of closed shops entitles a trade union to withdraw the card of a capable craftsman of good character who for years had been a member ... for any capricious reason ... is plainly in restraint of trade. At common law it is equally clearly unreasonable so far as the public interest is concerned. Is it then protected by either Section 3 or Section 4 of the Trade Union Act 1971? It cannot be said that a rule that enabled such capricious and despotic action is proper to the 'purposes' of this or indeed of any trade union. It is thus not protected by Section 3 and is moreover ultra vires. Nor can I find any protection for it in Section 4. It is thus ivitoid in restraint of trade.

The Irish Courts have been equally if not more explicit, a point which we shall develop in a moment.[29]

Let us pause at this point and consider the type of collectivity that attempts to exercise a pre-entry closed shop. A very prominent type of course is the craft union. A craft union differs from other unions in a number of important respects. It was the early form of trade union organisation. It set out to establish a relationship with a market rather than with a number of individual employers, that is to say it attempted to impose certain rules on the market. It did so in the following manner. It established a monopoly of the skill concerned and it tried to ensure that no one could exercise such a skill for gain in employment unless he was a member of the collectivity. This meant it could control the number of skilled persons entering the market, ensuring an adequate income for all. There were of course advantages for the employer as well since the trade union accepted substantial responsibility for maintaining a reasonable level of skill although, in time, this tended to deteriorate into a device for the postponing of young men entering the trade. It is not appropriate to consider in any depth the question of the craft union here. It is sufficient to recognise that, unlike other unions, the craft union sees the monopoly of skill as lying at the heart of its
78

ability to regulate the market and a monopoly of skill requires a disciplined and exclusive membership. It follows that a craft union will seek that no one but a member can be employed for gain to exercise that skill, and further, that if a member is expelled for any reason he is thereby excluded from the exercise of the skill. There are other trade unions which also tend to operate a pre-entry closed shop, prominent among them being British Actors Equity and the National Union of Journalists. Indeed the TUC campaign of non-registration under the 1971 Act caused considerable difficulty for British Actors Equity as a case in point.[30] Some raise the point, regarding these unions, that they are analogous to professions and in fact are exercising a professional function in relation to competence and control. Perhaps that is so. Clearly the craft union dilemma does appear to reflect a similar dilemma in the professional area and consequently it is necessary to spend a moment in considering such a similarity.

The term, profession, is often used loosely. We attribute the status of profession to accountants, to engineers and to economists. But if we are to make a comparison with craft unions then we must use it in a more rigorous way; we must use it only in respect of those bodies that set out in some sense to influence the market, that is to say, those bodies which appear to operate within a service monopoly, excluding from practice all except the members of the society concerned. Closely allied with this market regulation is the acceptance of responsibility for standards. Consequently a profession, defined in this more rigorous sense, is characterised by three functions, the function of regulating admission, the function of training and the function of supervision of performance. In Ireland, the two professions which most obviously exercise these functions are those of medicine and law.

As far as the first two functions are concerned, that of admission and that of training, there is much in common between the craft union and the profession. The function of regulating admission can ostensibly be justified on the grounds that only suitable people, in education and in character, should be accepted. This is still a critically important consideration for the professions. It was always less significant for the craft trades and is in any event much less

79

important now since the procedures developed by AnCO, the Industrial Training Authority, have greatly widened the scope of entry. Although capable of being justified in its own right, the regulation of entry can and is frequently used to limit the number of persons eventually entering the employment market. The same, broadly speaking, would apply to the function of training, the craft unions now playing a much more subsidiary part than they did in the past, but the professions still very influential both in the standard of courses and implicitly in the numbers entering the market. Of course there is cause for anxiety (and this was expressed by the Donovan Commission),[31] an anxiety that springs from a concern for the public interest and the general level of skill within the community where the market is so regulated. But to the jurist's mind, the question of the personal right which is invaded by the closed-shop does not turn on some general concern with the public interest but with an individual actually deprived.

It is in these circumstances that we turn to the third function, the function of supervision of performance. In the case of a profession, the deprivation of the right to engage in the work concerned arises largely because of malpractice and there is, in such cases, the right of appeal. In this matter the legal profession in Ireland is more autonomous than the medical profession but this difference need not delay us. The point to be made is that even in the case of the Incorporated Law Society exclusion from the profession for malpractice can be effected only by the High Court. In the case of a craft union, however, exclusion from the society may be effected for reasons quite unrelated to the manner in which the skill is discharged. A craftsman may be excluded from employment because, being a member of another union or being a member of none, he refuses to join the union that organises that employment; he may be excluded from employment because, being in dispute with the union, he is excluded from membership. The union does not justify its monopoly position as a profession does on the grounds that it is primarily in the business of guaranteeing a professional standard and will punish to the point of exclusion those who do not maintain it. It is bent on the general protection of its members' interests, although, as we shall later see, it is important

80

not to view this in too negative a light.

There are a number of positions one can take up therefore. One can take the view that, where it is not justified by its guaranteeing performance, such a monopoly is intrinsically wrong and should be condemned, or one can take the view that if one provided a system of appeal such as the professions have, then the practice can in fact be tolerated.

In the United Kingdom, courts on the whole appear to be of the opinion that a pre-entry closed shop in the manner which we have described it, is unlawful as being in restraint of trade. One scholar[32] in summarising the position has said:

> It is thought that the right to work is after all only a particular instance of the right to trade. To say that a rule is in restraint of the right to work is therefore tantamount to saying that it is in restraint of trade.

This indeed appears to be borne out in the various judgements. Lord Salmon in *Nagle's* case based his judgement on the leading case of *Nordenfelt v. Maxim Nordenfelt Guns and Ammunition Company*[33] where Lord MacNaghten said:

> All interference with individual liberty and trading and all restraints of trade of themselves, if there is nothing more, are contrary to public policy and therefore void. That is the general rule. But there are exceptions ...

But we must be cautious here. The common law does not speak merely of restraint of trade but rather of the unreasonable restraint of trade. Consequently, despite the vigour of the language, the judgements, including our earlier references to Salmon, L.J. and Sachs, J., do not exclude the idea of restraint in principle but rather exclude a restraint which is exercised capriciously and unjustly.

In Ireland the position appears to be somewhat more radical. The right to work is seen by the Irish courts to be fundamental. It is not stated explicitly in the Irish constitution, but in *Murtagh Properties* case[34] (and confirmed in Murphy's case)[35] the court held that there are, as we have already recognised, certain unspecified constitutional rights 'not confined to the rights specifically mentioned in the Constitution' but which 'may be derived from other clauses in the Constitution or from the Christian and democratic character of the state'. In *Murphy's* case Mr Justice

Walsh remarked that among the unspecified personal rights in the Constitution was the right to work, that is to say, the right not to be interfered with in one's capacity to earn one's living. It is not entirely clear whether this, although very radically put, excludes the pre-entry closed shop in principle. Mr Justice Walsh in *Murphy's* case appeared to contemplate some possibility of obliging a union in some circumstances to accept a person into membership, which in turn would imply some appellate system and would not necessarily exclude the principle of the pre-entry closed shop if the appellate system were satisfactory. But the better view seems to be that the court is concerned with the right to work, not the right to join an association, and its infringement appears to be seen as intrinsically wrong.

Having considered, then, the understanding of the courts in relation to where the limits lie in this area of trade union activity, let us consider the trade union's view of itself. A pre-entry closed shop, unlike a post-entry closed shop is espoused, as we have already remarked, only by a small number of trade unions and is not supported necessarily by the trade union movement as a whole. Therefore at the outset we must recognise some degree of uncertainty here.

But what of the craft union itself? What we say now does not necessarily apply to all craft trades but it does apply to a goodly number. Let us take account of the views not of the trade union leadership anxious about the survival of the organisation but rather, because it is where the vigour lies, the view of the community of craftsmen. They see themselves in peril. They see the peril arising in particular from technical change. In some instances technical innovation has greatly simplified that which in the past demanded considerable skill. In others, the skill has been so enhanced by technology that it has moved into the technician and quasi-professional field. There is also the threat from the employer, anxious to increase productivity and therefore prepared to fragment the skill and train unskilled workers to do specific aspects of it. If the trade union wishes to respond to its members in these circumstances it must resist technical change except where it is negotiated in what it regards as a satisfactory manner and it must resist as well any fragmentation of its central skill. But what does this mean in practice? It means that it must impose a penalty on any of its members who engage, without its consent, in new technical practices and it must require its members to refuse to work with such employees as can exercise only a limited aspect of the skill. If a member refuses to carry out its instructions then the penalty can be exclusion from the union and therefore exclusion from the right to work at the skill. This is where the crisis occurs. One can see readily enough that the survival which the community of craft workers wishes to attain can run headlong up against the right to work of an individual member of the craft.

Other trade unions, as we have noted, are somewhat reserved about all this. The acceptance of technical change in a particular employment may be a necessary price for the survival of the firm. While to a craftsman the maintenance of his market dominance may be more important than the survival of a particular firm, this is certainly not the case with many non-craft workers. Furthermore, the exclusivity of the craft union appears troublesome. Nevertheless, in the nature of things the other trade unions would not support any statutory intervention which would erode this power of market regulation. But their unease has nevertheless been expressed. It is reflected as we have seen in the establishment of the appeals board in 1964 by the Irish Congress of Trade Unions, which will hear appeals by individual members against their own unions in relation to expulsion. This however was as far as they were prepared to go.

Finally, with regard to this pre-entry closed shop, we come to the view of the public authority and here we find the debate presented in a very substantial way in the United Kingdom. Once again we find divided voices, reflecting the two major strands of British political life. The Donovan Commission was uneasy but not altogether prepared to condemn. Because, in their view, trade unions on the whole tended to act reasonably in this matter, they recommended not the abolition of the practice but rather a system of independent appeal and they were followed in this by the white paper, *In Place of Strife*, [36] where the safeguards suggested had two objectives, first to protect the freedom not to join a trade union on the part of a person with a conscientious difficulty, and second to give an individual protection against unfair or arbitrary action by a trade union. In both cases a system of independent adjudication was recommended with provision for damages.

But Conservative thinking found the idea of a pre-entry closed shop intolerable. They distinguished it from the post-entry closed shop which they described as a union shop and which they were prepared to tolerate in some degree; but the pre-entry closed shop was something to which they were fundamentally opposed.[37] This thinking found explicit expression in the Industrial Relations Act 1971 and it was made quite clear that in the matter of personal rights not only did there exist a right to belong to a trade union but also the right not to belong.[38] It followed therefore that pre-entry closed shop arrangements were rendered unlawful.

But the public authority does tend on the whole to take up a middle ground in such difficult matters. In the stormy events that followed the collapse of the Conservative government in 1974 there was an attempt by the Labour government to wipe the slate clean of all legislation in relation to the closed shop, but parliament, despite their wishes, re-enacted that part of the 1971 legislation which gave the individual the right to appeal to an independent tribunal if excluded from a trade union.[39] Clearly the Labour government of the time, despite their alliance with the TUC in this matter, were reluctant on the whole to go as far as the trade unions wished them to. This appears to be so, even though the provision was later repealed in 1976. On the other hand when the Conservative party returned to power, Mr Prior, the Employment Secretary, while reenacting the provision, did not make any substantial change in principle when eventually after much discussion he introduced his Employment Act in August 1980, although he strengthened the individual's position in a number of other ways. His successor, Mr Tebbitt, however, has taken a sterner line, very evident indeed in the Employment Act 1982.

There is in a word much uncertainty, much heart-searching, in this difficult area. Nor is it without passion, both in the strenuous desire of craft unions and professional unions to survive and in the equally passionate commitment of Conservative thinking to individual liberty despite the price that has to be paid.

The post-entry closed shop, that is to say, the arrangement under which the employee must join the appropriate trade union on his being employed or very shortly thereafter, does not raise as many difficulties as its pre-entry cousin. It is of course very widespread as a practice both in the United Kingdom and in Ireland. In 1964 the Donovan Commission found that two out of every five trade union members worked in a closed shop, by far the majority in such post-entry arrangements.

But what of the courts?[40] In the case of *Educational Company of Ireland Ltd. v. Fitzpatrick*[41] the issue turned on obliging an employee, to join a union, not on the point of his employment but well subsequent to that. It could not therefore be urged as a condition of his employment, and the endeavour on the part of the Irish national transport authority, CIE, to overcome the difficulty by disemploying all workers and re-employing them immediately subject to the new term was rejected by the courts as a device which did not change the essential character of the employment contract.[42] The same general view in regard to enforcing membership was taken more recently by the European Court of Human Rights.[43]

But what of the situation — which is quite widespread — where in a perfectly open way the employer, in pursuance of an agreement with a trade union, requires a new employee to become a member of the trade union concerned? If the employee chooses not to, then presumably he would not be offered the job, which in any event is a matter within the discretion of the employer. But what if later he chooses to dissociate himself from the union? If he is dismissed in these circumstances, is such a dismissal justified on the grounds that he has broken his contract, or is it the case that a fundamental right of dissociation is improperly invaded? It might be urged, for example, that membership of a voluntary association in a free society carries with it the right to evaluate and judge the performance of that association and that such an evaluation and such a judgement is not necessarily related, in the case of a trade union, to one's personal employment but rather to the character of the union and the persons who make it up. We have no secure

85

guidance on this from the Irish courts.

In the case of the public authority there is on the whole a view that the post-entry closed shop is benign, given that one provides for conscientious objection and fair dealing, and indeed we find the idea confirmed even under the 1971 Trade Union Act in the United Kingdom in the form of an agency shop. Moreover, employers as a whole, particularly when they employ large numbers, find the arrangement to be a useful one in that it tends to provide clarity in representation and stability in agreements. It may appear therefore that given certain safeguards, the post-entry closed shop has a good deal of consensual support. But this may be too bland a conclusion. Let us explore the question a little further by considering it from the point of view of the trade unions.

Since the idea of freedom of association became an issue in trade union disputes in Ireland, trade unions have tended to see it not as anything particularly fundamental but rather as another card to be played, a card which, if we are to follow the poker analogy, is the joker in the game when the joker is wild. This was abundantly clear in the first case in which the principle was raised, the *National Union of Railwaymen's* case,[44] where it would at first sight be quite proper to cast the NUR in the role of a liberal union determined to protect a citizen in his right to join and remain in the union of his choice. But some ten years earlier the same union was seen in the contrary role, where the High Court held against it for its part in greatly damaging the employment of a worker because he was not a member of the union.[45] However the dispute from the trade union point of view was the same in each case, a dispute in regard to jurisdiction between the National Union of Railwaymen and the Irish Transport and General Workers' Union, in which the highly sensitive question of British-based unions in Ireland was the central issue. The Irish Transport had fostered a breakaway union, the Federation of Road and Rail Workers, of which John Cooper was seen as a dangerous and disruptive protagonist, and consequently his appointment to areas where substantial numbers of NUR members were employed was resisted by that union. And when we turn to *NUR v. Sullivan* we find that the NUR sought relief from the activities essentially of the IT&GWU but specifically of a tribunal set up under the 1941 Trade Union Act which had the power to designate a single representative union in a particular employment in respect of which the NUR, because of its British base, was at a substantial disadvantage.[46] Neither the issue nor the protagonists had really changed from one case to the other, and therefore regarding the question as one of freedom of association gives a curiously false impression.[47]

It is important that we should see these jurisdictional disputes as clearly as possible, if only because they have been a considerable source of disputation. Since the issue of British-based unions in Ireland is no longer of major significance, the disputes have not in recent times sprung from trade union ambitions. They spring as a rule from disenchanted members, either because a union has given them bad service, or because they are an unlucky minority in a majority settlement. In such circumstances they may seek alternative trade union representation and as a consequence, if there is only one union in the job, may run up against the rules of good practice which govern unions affiliated to the Irish Congress of Trade Unions. This is an area of difficulty, and has resulted in union suspensions and withdrawals from Congress. The number of unions who now lie outside Congress on this account is not large, but they are an uncontrolled refuge for disaffected members of other unions, and a steady source of industrial disputes. Here the endeavours of the Congress to maintain some order and discipline are of course of great importance, but they are endeavours which confront rather uneasily the principle of freedom of association.

The second great dispute area where freedom of association is unhappily called into play is the area of non-recognition, that is to say where an employer refuses to recognise a trade union or, where he does, conducts himself in a reluctant and uncooperative manner. We have already taken note of this in our reference to *Educational Company of Ireland v. Fitzpatrick*.[48] We have seen too that the object of the union members in that case was not to invade any constitutional rights of their fellow workers but to survive themselves in an employment where the employer was understood to be hostile to trade union organisation. But a more frequent example of non-recognition arises not from any bloodymindedness on the part of the employer but rather from a dispute between some employees and the union already recognised by the employer, where they seek to be represented by an alternative union. This in fact is more properly a variation of a jurisdictional dispute, although in practice it must also be acknowledged that there are many instances where the employer is far from being an innocent bystander. How far freedom of association is a real issue in all this is difficult to say.

Nor should a mean-minded reluctance to share in the financing of a trade union masquerade as a great constitutional freedom. If such an issue is to be pleaded then it should be properly grounded, however difficult this might be, and this was clearly the intention in the United Kingdom in the provision for conscientious objection and the agency shop.

Indeed the only case in Ireland where the principle of freedom of association was explicitly and wholly relevant was *Meskell v. CIE*[49] a case that arose from the ill-fated attempt to re-employ all employees on a new contract which would include a trade union membership clause and which a prominent member of long-standing objected to on the grounds of principle. Both CIE and the Irish Transport and General Workers' Union did all they could to avoid the confrontation, sensing their vulnerability on the issue, quite correctly as events showed.

Where then does the conflict of view, the normative disagreement, lie in this area of closed shops and we must for the purposes of the question have regard to the whole closed-shop area, whether pre-entry or post-entry? It appears that it is the right to work that is called into play in the case of the pre-entry closed shop, while freedom of association appears to be the issue in post-entry cases. This can be seen more clearly if we regard the pre-entry closed shop as being directed ad hominem, since an actual person, in his acceptability to the union, is the subject of the dispute, while the post-entry closed shop is primarily directed *ad rem,* the res in this case being the general rule of membership in respect of which all employees are broadly treated alike. It is not surprising then that in the case of the right to work, there is an acceptance by the trade union of the principle, and an acceptance as well of the relevance of that principle as a limitation on its activities. Certain unions may challenge its conclusiveness in their own case, but the trade union movement as a whole is uneasy when challenged with its breach. In the case of freedom of association, however, and in particular where it applies to the post-entry closed shop, while the principle is accepted by the trade unions, its relevance is denied, at least in the vast majority of cases. This is because freedom of association implies the invasion of a personal right, yet as a rule no invasion of a personal right is contemplated. It is essentially *ad rem*. It concerns a straightforward recognition dispute, or a jurisdictional dispute between two unions. It is here, I believe, that the unions would claim that the courts should take account of the overriding intention of the parties, rather than seeing the principle stand as a barrier in all cases.

But there may be a further reason for the barrier, representing a deeper normative divide. We find for example in the *Report of the Commission of Inquiry on Industrial Relations*[50] that while the commissioners accepted in principle the immunities in relation to industrial action, requiring essentially that proper procedures should be followed, they recommended the withdrawal in an absolute fashion of the immunities in the case of recognition disputes and in the case of disputes between unions. This was puzzling in view of the fact that they had clearly both accepted and developed the distinction between disputes as to interest and disputes as to rights, submitting only the latter to some judicial process but they nevertheless excluded disputes on trade union recognition and trade union jurisdiction. They did not claim that these were disputes as to rights, since manifestly they could not be, and the reasons they did offer appear superficial and poorly argued. It would not be unfair to conclude that there was seen to be some fundamental impropriety in the fact that disputes which arise among members of a trade union (since this is frequently the case with recognition disputes as well) should be given any standing, that there was some fundamental illegitimacy in this kind of activity that should not be recognised by the law.

Once again one is tempted to the view that when normative differences arise in industrial relations they arise in the area of the freedoms of a trade union and the rights of which it stands possessed. It is not merely a question of the common law courts being unable to see a collectivity as it would see a natural person. It is somewhat more profound. There still lingers in the general mind a reserve about the fundamental legitimacy of a trade union, and therefore a tendency to see it, not as possessed naturally of certain freedoms and rights, but rather as having these, in some limited way, conferred on it, and therefore open to change or withdrawal as the public interest might require without any necessary invasion of some antecedent right such as a natural person possesses.

Before we leave the question of workers' rights and the manner, in which they might be invaded by a trade union, let us consider briefly what has been described as natural justice, and although this applies to employers no less than trade unions and indeed to all who exercise a judicial function, it manifests itself, in industrial relations, particularly in the manner in which trade unions deal with their internal disputes.

We are in the area here where the trade union as a domestic tribunal imposes a penalty on a member and the manner in which such a function may properly be carried out. We find no definition of natural justice in statute, but it is a matter on which the common law has a good deal to say. If a domestic tribunal acts in a manner contrary to natural justice, the courts may intervene to set the matter to rights, even where the action of the tribunal is in accord with the union's own rules.[51] But in what does this idea of natural justice consist?

Lord Pearse in *Faramus v Film Artistes Association*[52] has recourse to Lord Russell in an early case[53] concerning the propriety of certain bye-laws and in following Lord Russell would consider certain matters contrary to natural justice

if for instance they were found to be partial and unequal in their operation as between different classes; if they were manifestly unjust; if they disclosed bad faith; if they involved an oppressive and gratuitous interference with the rights of those subject to them as could find no justification in the minds of reasonable men ...

Bryn Perrins[54] summarises more soberly his understanding of natural justice under English law as follows:

90

It is said that where a tribunal exercises a judicial or similar function, that is, when it decides people's rights, then that tribunal must observe the rules of natural justice, and those rules are that a person whose rights are affected had
—the right to have his case tried by an unbiassed tribunal;
—the right to have adequate notice of any charges against him;
—the right to put his case to the tribunal.

It does appear that in the dictum of Lord Pearse there are certain substantive issues of importance, issues which call for such phrases as 'manifestly unjust', 'bad faith' and 'interference with personal right', and of course the term 'natural justice' itself gives rise to ideas of a moral and ethical kind which we discussed earlier in relation to natural law. Perrins, on the other hand, offers conditions which are essentially procedural in character. And it does appear that in practice the notion of natural law exaggerates the idea. Indeed it seems to me that we can follow Perrins in the matter and regard natural justice as springing not from natural law, not from some substantive base in morality, but rather from procedural requirements. It does seem at first sight to be an exercise in reductionism to speak merely of consistency when much more vigorous and promising words such as fairness are in play; but when we examine the circumstances in which this problem has arisen and in particular the various judgements of the courts, we find that indeed consistency of rule is the central theme. It is evident in the general prohibition against being partial and unequal as between classes, in the requirement that a tribunal should be unbiassed and in the requirement that an opportunity must be given to a man to refute a charge brought against him, to put his own case and to have adequate notice.

Natural justice then, understood as Lord Sachs understood it as fair play in action,[55] cannot be seen in practice as importing more than this requirement for rule consistency; it need not be, and is not in the industrial relations context, associated with any great ethical principle which transcends the rules of adjudication, but rather springs from the nature of the rules themselves. In such circumstances one would not anticipate any great conflict between the various parties on what is right and what is just; and yet as far as trade unions are concerned there is a certain area of tension.

91

We have already seen that trade unions tend to regard themselves as comprehensive democratic societies, and therefore appeals by members against decisions of the union must be satisfied within the structure. And yet as the Donovan Commission pointed out[56] it can be said that when a trade union, through some committee of its own, sits in judgement upon a member, 'it is in effect acting as judge and jury in its own cause.' As a consequence of this we find that in the United Kingdom there was much discussion and also statutory provision with the object of regulating trade unions in their domestic affairs, and although a trade union accepts that members may appeal to a court of law against its decision, to import into its domestic rules and practices provisions which are not decided on democratically is quite another matter. Since this is in effect intervention by the public authority in the public interest (although of course not exclusively so) we shall take up the topic in the next chapter.

Let us turn now to the situatuion of the employer in the face of trade union activity, the rights of the employer and the manner in which they might be invaded. We can divide the discussion into two areas, his rights in his property and his rights in his trade.

The question of property rights appears at first sight to be the more straightforward. The obvious way in which they can be affected in an industrial dispute is by the act of picketing. If we were to look merely at the tradition of the common law we would find picketing to be, in itself, of doubtful legality, although there was a view that peaceful communication by attending at or near a person's premises might be regarded as a freedom under the common law.[57] In the United Kingdom however it now appears to be the case that even one person engaging peacefully in picketing is committing a common law nuisance, and it is likely that the courts in Ireland would take a similar view. However, so powerful and obvious a trade union tradition is picketing that the public authority has for many years taken a contrary view and has endeavoured to give the practice protection in the special circumstances of industrial disputes. It is of course recognised to be something of a special licence for trade unions, a licence, in common law terms, to beset a man's premises, in contradiction of his right to quiet enjoyment, and therefore when the statute comes under the eye of the court it is seen not to change the thrust of the law, not to legitimate what before was wrongful, but rather to make a limited rule for limited circumstances. It followed, not unnaturally, that the courts, conscious of what they saw as the aberrant nature of the provision, sought to limit its effect as much as possible, and for many years this was a marked characteristic of Irish judicial practice, much more so than in the United Kingdom. Indeed in one case, where an employer made his employees co-directors of a company created for the purpose so that the strike could no longer be regarded as a trade dispute nor picketing rendered immune, the judge, in holding for the employer, said that while the formation of the company might have been a subterfuge 'the question which I must determine is whether it is a successful subterfuge ... a very net point, a technical one perhaps, but the whole subject is itself rather technical.'[58] This excessive legalism is perhaps not so evident today, but it has created in the trade union mind a belief that in trade union matters the courts were not only prejudiced but perverse.[59]

The employer, although profoundly resentful of picketing, tends as a rule to view the question once again in a practical way. He recognises that in the courts he will find on the whole a sympathetic ear, but common sense indicates that there is little point in taking proceedings in regard to picketing if relations are gravely damaged by so doing, and in particular if the issue is not likely to be heard for many months. There have been many instances in Ireland where workers mounted pickets in disputes which clearly were not within the statutory definition of a trade dispute[60] and yet the employer did not find it expedient to take action. On the other hand, the employer in Ireland in particular has found in the labour injunction a useful and immediate instrument for restraining picketing and the confusion in the minds of the High Court judges regarding the grounds on which interlocutory labour injunctions should be granted has not helped matters.[61]

This tendency to the expedient on the part of the employer is evident in the Report of the Irish Commission of Inquiry on Industrial Relations[62] which must be regarded, at least as far as the

93

majority opinion is concerned, as an employer view, since the trade union representatives withdrew from the Commission at quite an early stage. There, picketing is not excluded although the immunity is much circumscribed by a circumscribing of the area within which a trade dispute is legitimate. More than that — and this indeed emphasises the employer's anxiety to retain discretion in how he might approach such matters — there is no suggestion that offences of a criminal kind should be erected. It is merely proposed that such actions could, in the hands of the employer, be open to an application for a labour injunction or be grounds for the recovery of damages.

There is much uneasiness among trade unions in relation to picketing as well, probably because of the uncertain grounds of licence on which it rests. There is no doubt that peaceful picketing is seen as an essential instrument, indeed the primary one, in an industrial dispute. Its effectiveness lies not merely in peaceful communication but in the fact that workers will not pass it and therefore will withdraw from their employment. Of course it relies for this effectiveness on the loyalty of the workers one to another, and the loyalty frequently of other workers who have no direct relationship with the dispute. On the other hand, such loyalty, instant and unquestioning (certainly at the outset), makes trade unions, no less than employers, vulnerable to spontaneous, irresponsible and unauthorised pickets, and this was very much the case in Ireland during the 1960s and for much of the 1970s as well. A picket appeared to command workers of all unions, not merely members of the union in dispute, and much industrial disruption followed.[63] It was in these circumstances that in 1970 Congress adopted what it described as its picketing policy. The problem that was addressed was a severe one, because to decry picketing — if such were done — would be to decry trade union solidarity. Yet some clarification and discipline were essential. It was decided to establish a device called an all-out picket, which every trade union member, and not only members of the disputing union, had to observe. But such an all-out picket could be granted only by the Congress on application from the union concerned and after consultation with all the other unions involved. Of course in the

94

ordinary way, pickets are placed merely by the union directly in dispute, and in such circumstances, which represent very much the majority, the picket was deemed to apply to members of that union only and to no other.

It is interesting to consider the grounds on which an all-out picket is now granted by the Irish Congress of Trade Unions. The consent of all the other unions involved is not a requirement, although they must be consulted. The judgement of Congress itself is the key, and this judgement once again appears to be based on quite pragmatic considerations such as the likelihood of bringing the dispute to a rapid conclusion. The Congress is reluctant to enter into the merits of the dispute, and in this way it preserves for each union its independence and discretion, an idea that is central to the idea of the Congress in any event.

In summary then the trade union view appears to be that the picket as an instrument must be preserved, that it is vulnerable as a device, particularly if it is used with manifest irresponsibility, and therefore some orderliness is necessary for its preservation, but this orderliness should be secured without damage to the essential freedom of the trade union. Although in practice there is concern for the employer and his rights in the matter, the motivation for good order does not primarily spring from this.

This then is an area of no little difficulty. There is little doubt that on all sides picketing is seen as an invasion of some rights of an employer. On the other hand it is traditionally seen by the trade unions as a special freedom which they possess, and this the public authority is prepared to accept in some measure and provide for by statute. The courts while applying the statute law are restless in regard to the manner in which it appears to contradict the traditions of the common law, and in the light of all this, there appears to be some pressure, not only among employers but among many others as well, for some further limitation of the circumstances in which lawful picketing may take place without discounting the freedom itself.[64] It is a limitation which trade unions certainly in Ireland would vigorously resist, and it is for that reason that we must recognise in this area substantial conflict in the notion of obligation and right.

But let us suppose that workers go further than picketing. There have, in recent times, been instances where workers have chosen to sit-in either in the pursuance of a dispute or, as is more often the case, in protest at a closure which failed to recognise their interests. This of course is trespass; it is clearly contrary to law, and is usually a spontaneous act which has not the union's authority. It is not legitimated by tradition as picketing in some measure appears to be, and therefore might be regarded as being no more a subject of normative controversy than common assault which may also arise during an industrial dispute and which would be condemned by all. In the formal sense therefore there seems to be no conflict here. And yet some caution is necessary.

There has developed since the last war a deeper vision of the rights of a worker. It was to be seen first in the notion of statutory compensation for redundancy and then in provisions against unfair dismissal which, in the United Kingdom and in Ireland, shifted the burden for demonstrating right action substantially towards the employer. This, as we have already seen, means that while before an employer could dismiss a worker in accordance with his contract unless the worker could prove malice or some other form of wrongdoing on the part of the employer, now the procedure swings the other way, and we find, in the general thrust of the legislation, that the worker may claim to continue in his employment, despite the provisions as to notice, unless the employer can show that the dismissal was because of redundancy or because of wrongdoing on the part of the worker himself. This of course raises the question of what right it is that shelters behind these somewhat complex provisions. Of course, some would claim that all this merely reflected the luxury of a high-employment economy, a yielding to populist pressures without any great consideration of the principles involved, but on the other hand there were those who saw in it some burgeoning of the idea of a worker's right in his employment, more fundamental and more extensive than a contractual right. It was suggested that it was perhaps analogous to a trader's goodwill, or perhaps analagous to a property right of some kind; but some took the question further and began to see it not merely as analagous to a property right but an actual form of that right. Indeed the same idea seems to underlie the notion of worker directors, a particular form of industrial democracy which goes well beyond what is necessary to promote higher productivity or better work relations. In its more highly developed form of co-determination, in the Federal Republic of Germany, it was challenged in the Federal Constitutional Court on these grounds among others, that, in a word, the property of the firm was lodged in the shareholders and co-determination invaded such a property right. But the Federal Constitutional Court found for the legislation, and in brief were of the view, in a very lengthy judgment,[65] that while a minority shareholder could require the prudent use of his investment, he could command no more. It appears that workers' property rights in the firm are not dissimilar in kind, each worker commanding no more than the prudent protection of his employment but together, just as shareholders do, expressing this by way of representative involvement in the direction of the firm, creating a constitutency of equal status with that of the shareholders. This too appears to be echoed in Pope John Paul's remarkable *Laborem Exercens*.[66] While in the United Kingdom these ideas would still be regarded as somewhat implausible, they have had perhaps a wider acceptance in Ireland, although by no means a substantial one. This was reflected in the manner in which the Irish Minister for Labour presented his bill which later became the Workers' Participation (State Enterprises) Act. While he hoped from the bill (which provided for worker directors in certain state companies) an improvement in efficiency and better work attitudes, such arguments clearly had a secondary place; the principal reason for the proposal was that it was right,[67] and although the argument was not developed, the same implication of a personal right in employment remained. Nor could the matter really be pursued further. Employers opposed the extension of the idea by statute to the private sector, claiming that each firm should develop it as it thought fit. This in effect meant that the question was one of discretion for the employer, not of right for the worker, but while that would still appear to be the strong general view, the notion of a right persists, and seems to be present in the sit-ins which have occurred in Ireland.

During 1982 and early 1983 these were quite dramatic. Some were injuncted, leading, when the workers refused to obey the court orders, to imprisonment and the threat of imprisonment. Although some of this may have been deliberately contrived by the workers for publicity purposes, a great deal of it represented a sense of outrage that there should be such apparent disregard for workers' rights in the lay-offs and closures which gave rise to the disputes. If one reflects on what rights were actually being urged it is difficult to avoid the notion of a property right, at least as compelling as an easement of some kind. It would certainly be wrong to see it as merely a contractual right supplemented by certain statutory supports which have welfare as their objective.

In general however trade unions no less than the government have viewed this development very uneasily and while campaigning quite properly for some amendment of company law, they have recognised, at least privately, that legitimating trespass (or, implicitly, damage to property) in the furtherance of a trade dispute is quite another matter. But although there is uneasy and inarticulate leadership in the evolution of this right in Ireland, it would I think be unwise to set it aside. Yet so profoundly does it contradict the understanding of most employers regarding the very nature of ownership, that it is quite likely to give rise in the future to normative conflict.

We now turn to an employer's rights in his trade, and how a trade union might invade such rights in the course of its activities. But what are these rights and how are they to be expressed? If I, as a trader, compete with another, and, because I have greater resources and can buy more cheaply, I put him deliberately out of business, I contravene no right of his in the present convention of trade. If I am genuinely pursuing my own interest then the harm I may do him as a consequence is neither here nor there. Why then should not a collectivity, pursuing prmarily its own interest, be seen in the same light? Indeed there was a time when the courts appeared to admit this argument.[68] The general view, however, is that this is not the settled law in the matter. But why should this be the case?

It is necessary first to be clear on the kind of trade union activity we have in mind. This is essentially a strike, or indeed the threat of a strike. Let us set aside for the moment such ancillary activities as picketing, which may be of questionable legality, and speak only of a group of workers withdrawing from their employment in order to bring pressure on an employer to concede a claim of theirs. What rights then does this activity invade?

The courts have consistently condemned what they describe as restraint of trade, but only in circumstances where it is unreasonable. But this exonerates a trader who, by vigorous competition, excludes another from trading when his purpose is primarily to benefit himself. It does not make clear why a collectivity should not be exonerated when its purpose too is primarily to benefit itself. Furthermore what we are speaking of here is a freedom to trade, and as we have seen we are in the difficulty that a freedom as such has no correlative obligation.[69] For this we must seek out not the freedom but the right of the trader, a right explicit enough to impose an obligation on others. A concept such as the unreasonable restraint of trade does not therefore bring us very far. Let us have regard instead to statute and the rights which are there conferred on the trader; and having identified such rights as exist generally, let us go on to examine how they assist us in understanding the trade union position. We take the Irish statutes for the purpose since they will serve as well as another.

The Mergers, Take-Overs and Monopolies (Control) Act of 1978 provides for the identification of those traders who wholly or largely dominate or threaten to dominate a market and sets out to evaluate the consequences of their activities and if necessary curb them. The primary objective here appears to be the protection of the consumer rather than other traders. Much the same can be said of the provisions against the abuse of patent monopoly rights under the Patents Act of 1964, and price control legislation has the same objective. All this however does not help us very much in clarifying the rights of the trader as distinct from the consumer. For this we can turn to the Restrictive Practices Act 1972, which appears to have such an objective in mind.

There are in Irish practice no *per se* offences against the canons of competition and fair trading (and Ireland is exceptional in this);

instead specific prohibitions are made after inquiry which apply only to the trade or service in question.[70] Since these prohibitions tend to repeat themselves they are as revealing for our purpose as the per se prohibitions in other countries.

The prohibitions that emerge clearly enough are retail price maintenance (with some correlative concern about excessive price cutting), horizontal price fixing and discrimination in supply against particular retailers, all being arrangements among suppliers; in addition, there are prohibitions on restriction on entry to trade, market sharing and exclusive dealing, these being arrangements among traders in general, but often among retailers, and in particular expressed through trade associations.[71] The common characteristic here is that of joint action against an individual, and this really appears to be the nub of the question. It must be distinguished from a situation where an individual trader competes with another individual to his eventual exclusion. It would appear that the nature of the trade which is being protected, the nature of the trade which is regarded as benign and desirable, is one of individual competitiveness. Indeed the early American anti-trust legislation has been characterised as the defence of the corner store. It is this that the courts as a whole regard as being worthy of defence.

But where then is the trader's right? It probably does not spring from him personally at all but rather from the rules which by common consent are deemed necessary in order to protect that kind of market within which individual competitiveness can flourish. These consensual rules, recognised by the common law courts, predated the statutory rules which we have just described; but they arose primarily for reasons of public interest rather than personal vindication.

What then of trade unions? It is true of course that in Ireland 'services provided under a contract of employment' are excluded from the effect of the restrictive practices legislation;[72] nevertheless the primary significance of individual competitiveness, which the act enshrines, informs not only judicial thinking but society generally, making trade union action by way of organised withdrawal of labour somewhat perilous, principally because it is a

100

collective act. Once again however the powerful trade union tradition of freedom to strike tended to prevail with the public authority, and it was given specific protection in the circumstances of a trade dispute.

It might be urged that there is a deeper legitimacy that a trade union can call on for its collective efforts on behalf of its members other than merely the sanction of tradition. Socialist thinking — and indeed that form of it which so profoundly influenced trade unions in these islands — held that the means of production should be lodged in the hands of the public authority and trading carried out by local societies of a cooperative character. This indeed is a profound alternative to the individual competitiveness which we speak of here. But although trade union leaders may on occasion speak warmly of such an alternative, they do not recognise in it a plausible ground of right, except perhaps for the purposes of rhetoric. On the whole the trade unions appear to accept a society where, in private trading in any event, individual competitiveness is the touchstone, and if it is to be opposed, they oppose it not on the grounds of any great socialist ideal but simply on the grounds of a traditional freedom of a trade union to take strike action.

The situation is therefore not dissimilar to that of picketing, although the tendency of the courts to tight construction is less marked, largely because, not being so clearly unlawful in common law terms, strike action earns a somewhat greater indulgence.

5

The institution which we call upon to vindicate a right is essentially a judicial one. There are two things which we must note about such vindications, the first being that we see here applied a rule that has been determined on, at least in general, before the trial of the dispute, and the second being that there can be only one final judgement, one right answer. Of course there may be many opinions on what is right and much debate about the propriety of the answer that is handed down, but these are opinions and debates merely; only one answer can stand when the full judicial process has been completed. All this is very different from the type of institution which is appropriate to a dispute of interest where no rights are involved. This, as we have already recognised, raises no little difficulty for a trade union.

The validity of the rule in the first instance and the acceptance of its application, that is to say the judgement, in the second, rely, as we have seen, on consensus or normative agreement. In other words, there must be ultimate commitment on the part of both parties, however difficult the decision, to the support of the rule and to the support of the institution that applies it. But we have seen in the case of a trade union that the freedoms which it pursues and the rights which it claims are by no means generally accepted, particularly in the traditions of the common law, and, on the other hand, the trade unions themselves view the courts with a great deal of reserve.

These are the dilemmas facing one in the creation of appropriate judicial institutions to deal with labour disputes. In the United Kingdom there has been much debate and experimentation in this area, and some debate as well, although on a minor level, in Ireland. These questions however apply to all disputes as to rights, including such rights as may be erected by the intervention of the public authority itself. This latter is the subject of the next chapter and we shall therefore postpone a consideration of judicial institutions until such time as we have explored this final area.

CHAPTER FOUR

Obligations arising from Public Authority Intervention

1

We are concerned in this chapter with the government and the legislature, and the manner in which they intervene in industrial relations. And primarily we are concerned with formal obligation. What we have in mind then is the making of a law or a rule by the public authority and its enforcement, which in turn of course implies both a judicial process and the existence of a system of sanction. And yet if we were to deal only with this aspect of the public authority's role in industrial relations we should give a distorted and inadequate picture, because the reality is that governments in more recent times tend to see their role primarily as fostering and facilitating good industrial relations, in which of course regulation has an essential part, but not necessarily the most significant one.

A great deal of this arose from the special position which trade unions attained in these islands in the years since 1946. In the political circumstances of the time trade unions were seen as having a creative contribution to make to the rebuilding of economies, and the notion of their being to some degree partners in a great national developmental enterprise found its flowering in Ireland in the brief and false summer of the late forties and in particular in the Industrial Efficiency and Prices Bill of 1947 which provided for a number of major reforms including development councils in industry in which trade unions would have a part.[1] But the measure was before its time; the government that sponsored it went out of office and its successor did not pursue the matter. Ireland collapsed into the economic doldrums of the fifties and the more advanced proposals of the bill did not see implementation until the 1960s.

When, in those early years, the state turned to strictly labour matters, they naturally espoused the idea of facilitation rather than regulation, confident that once adequate structures were created the good sense of both parties would prevail and good industrial relations would be ensured. This indeed was the character of the Industrial Relations Act 1946 under which the Labour Court was established, and while the measure had limited regulative functions its primary purpose was to facilitate; again and again in the debates in parliament leading up to its enactment this point was made.[2] In the late sixties there was an unhappy attempt to assemble these two ideas of economic partnership and self-regulation in industrial relations in a single institutional form,[3] in a word in a system which would integrate prices and incomes in a single coherent policy, which, despite goodwill, was for the trade unions insupportable in principle.[4] Instead, the notion of partnership, which still to some degree prevailed, resulted in a very successful development in the national management of incomes, the series of national pay agreements of the nineteen seventies.[5] The position of the government in relation to them was somewhat ambivalent in the early years, but in what were described as the national understandings of 1979 and again of 1980[6] we see some strong indication of a tripartite partnership, employer, trade union and government, involving in the bargaining not only pay but, significantly, governmental matters such as taxation and the allocation of resources for employment purposes.

This system now seems largely to have come to an end. The employers, the trade unions and the government seem to have drawn back (as they appear to have in Europe generally)[7] into a stakeholder posture, making experiments of a joint management kind difficult and in any event largely unattractive, but there still remain the echoes of a large and national consensus.

The development in the United Kingdom was more extreme, holding out, at the outset, very much more hope of partnership and ending in the present year of 1983, with a degree of combativeness, with a degree of institutional hostility, not experienced in Ireland. The immense contribution of the British labour movement during the war and in particular to the post-war reconstruction of Europe gave it considerable prestige and a new status politically which made plausible the notion of economic partnership, giving rise to the various planning and administrative bodies and, in the sixties in particular, to the institutions for the national management of prices and incomes, which Ireland unsuccessfully attempted to imitate.

In the more domestic area of industrial disputes there was, in such a climate, and in a far more comprehensive way than in Ireland, a desire to respect the good sense of employer and trade union, to respect what was described as free collective bargaining. The public authority therefore, instead of busying itself distantly with regulation (as had been its major concern in earlier years) sought, not surprisingly, to facilitate the development of such a view and to confirm the idea of free collective bargaining as the underlying principle upon which good industrial relations rested.

When this rather noble partnership vision broke up in the late sixties the essential good sense of free collective bargaining still prevailed and the need for its facilitation. We see it, despite the robust conflicts of Conservative and Labour, in the various policy documents which were published at the time. It is true that there was much difference of emphasis; it is true that the Conservative party was impatient to use regulation where this seemed appropriate, convinced that a government should 'not just sit on the sidelines — exhorting people to change their attitudes and habits and providing voluntary conciliation machinery when disputes arise.'[8] Yet all this was still in the context of free collective bargaining, and we find later in the Guide to the Industrial Relations Act 1971 a statement to the effect that the purpose of the act was to promote good industrial relations in accordance with a number of general principles, the first being 'freely conducted collective bargaining which pays due regard to the community's general interest.'[9] The present Conservative government, since taking office, seems to have wholly rejected in policy matters such remnants of trade union partnership as might have remained and indeed to have adopted also an unusually negative approach to trade unions, expressing itself in a series of regulative measures which we shall later discuss. The facilitation and fostering of good industrial relations are not now the dominant objectives. It would appear however that this development, which has echoes of an earlier period, is an unusual one and does not reflect general European trends.

But all this had a perhaps not unexpected consequence. Trade unions could no longer be dismissed as something peripheral to the welfare of society, and when the days of social partnership fell away their importance did not diminish, but rather, certainly in Conservative eyes, they began to be seen as threatening and disruptive. It is not surprising therefore that we see, even among those who would hold the middle ground, a concern for their regulation.

The Donovan Commission Report set the scene well. It remarked that the distinctive feature of the British industrial relations system — up to that point — was that the state in the regulatory sense remained aloof even to the point of ensuring by statute that bargains made between employers and trade unions were not directly enforceable.[10] And while this policy concerned principally relations between employer and trade union, the statute also applied to certain relations between a member and his trade union.[11] But of course while the state, through its regulations, remained aloof the common law did not. Up to the time of the Donovan Commission report, the question for debate really turned on the extent to which this non-interventionist policy of the state should operate so as to limit the enthusiasm of the common law.

Now, however, the Donovan Commission raised the question whether this abstentionist policy should be abandoned, that is to say the question of the propriety of intervention by statute no less than the common law in industrial relations and in particular in trade union affairs. The question was also discussed in the policy documents of the two political parties of much the same time *Fair Deal at Work*[12] and *In Place of Strife*[13] with much concurrence in principle. For the first time, the use of statute was proposed not merely to provide a framework for resolving disputes, not merely to set aside the more onerous effects of court decisions, but actually to attempt to oversee and regulate the manner in which, in particular, trade unions conducted their business. Neither was it just a

106

negative approach, the undoing of certain statutory indemnifications which trade unions enjoyed, although this too was proposed. What we find is a positive act of intervention in trade union affairs on the grounds of public interest. This idea found its full flowering in the Industrial Relations Act 1971, and while the Labour party, on returning to office in 1974, dispatched the measure comprehensively, their earlier document, *In Place of Strife*, showed a disposition for regulation, particularly in the proposals on registration, although they were milder and less ambitious. On the other hand, the trade unions found the development wholly improper and quite insupportable, and it is against such a background of what appears as an unbridgeable divide, must we consider the question of institutions.

Before we go on to consider regulation, that is to say the formal imposition of obligation by the public authority, there are three further points which we should make in an endeavour to clear the ground for a more precise discussion of the nature of public regulation in industrial relations and its legitimacy. The three points concern first the ability of the government to influence without regulation, second the character of a political strike, and third the role of the government as an employer.

It is of course obvious enough that a government, in order to have its way in national economic matters, does not necessarily have to rely on regulation. It carries itself very great influence. This is so in particular in the case of the employer, who finds himself often a substantial client of the government's in a variety of ways.[14] Furthermore the government itself being an employer of considerable magnitude can influence conclusively national pay levels. This indeed was the case in the final stages of the negotiation on the second national understanding in Ireland, where the Taoiseach impatient for an agreement informed the employers that unless they met the trade union position, the government would come to agreement as the dominant employer in the public sector, leaving the private employers with no practical alternative.

The second point concerns the so-called political strike. In Ireland there has been growing restlessness among those in the PAYE sector, that is to say employees generally, concerning the burden of direct taxation which they believe to be inequitable and which they primarily must carry. In March 1983 clerical workers in a large firm in the south of Ireland, operating within a union shop situation, refused to make the tax and social welfare deductions, acting in consort with the workers generally who were demanding their full pay. There was some accommodation made by the firm of a non-committal kind, but this strike against tax alarmed the general trade union movement, who, in attempting to gain control of the developing unrest, called a half-day strike which was well supported. It could be urged that this was not an intervention by government in industrial relations but the very contrary. One could suggest that it was not a trade union matter at all, but merely the abuse of the trade union instrument for a political purpose. But this rather begs the question. It does appear that once the government permits tax to be made a significant part of national pay bargaining, as indeed it did in the national pay agreements in 1979 and 1980, one invites such a development. At that time workers were encouraged to have regard not to the gross level of pay but to what they took home. This was urged in particular by the employers, who, with some reason, believed that increases given by them, and heavily taxed subsequently, had merely the effect of increasing their costs while in no way adequately satisfying workers' demands. If then the government in its tax policy could be involved in the deal the problem might be handled in a more reasonable fashion. But once tax was seen not as a discretionary act of the government as a sovereign but as something which was open to a bargain and therefore to industrial coercion, the possibility of a tax strike was made far more plausible. We mention this merely in passing; it still lies somewhat outside the scope of industrial relations as such.

The third point runs as follows. In all this we have been considering, *inter alia*, the activities of the government *qua* government, but the government in its own right as a considerable employer is just as likely to fall into dispute as any other employer. It is nonetheless the government, and the question that arises therefore is whether those in dispute with it have less legitimacy in what they do than if they were in dispute with a private employer. A further question, deriving probably from the first, is whether or not the government may call to its aid certain powers of enforcement which it as a government possesses but which would not be possessed by a private employer. At the heart of these questions lies the status of a civil service association or union and the extent to which its freedom to act is constrained.

Let us for this purpose pursue events as they occurred in Ireland. Something of the attitude of the government to this problem in the immediate post-war years is seen in the Industrial Relations Act of 1946 where under section 4 civil servants, and certain other public authority officials, were excluded from access to the Labour Court, a matter to which we have already referred in our discussion on third party institutions. It was widely recognised that the Taoiseach of the time, Mr de Valera, took the view that civil servants could not engage in industrial action because to do so would be to enter into dispute not with an employer but with the people of Ireland. It is difficult to know how widely this view was held in the Ireland of the time.[15] In any event civil servants never contemplated strike action; it was beyond the horizons of plausibility. All this we have already noted. Moreover, un-authorised absence, even to the extent of a single day, rendered nugatory all the superannuation credits which a civil servant had built up to that point, and this of course greatly reinforced the implausibility of strike action. However the very much more abrasive years of the 1970s saw a great deal of militancy developing particularly in the Department of Posts and Telegraphs among lower paid workers resulting in a number of stoppages, some of great length and bitterness. In the Irish courts' interpretation of the Trade Disputes Act 1906 employees such as civil servants were excluded from the benefit of the immunities of the act on the grounds that they were not engaged in trade or industry and therefore were not workers in accordance with the act's definitions. Despite extensive picketing, however, the government at no time availed of the powers it had either to injunct or to sue subsequently for damages. Indeed if anything their inclination appeared to be to place, as far as possible, these employees on the same basis as employees in the private sector. In the early 1970s we find that the

109

civil service pension scheme was amended so that breaks in service no longer had a devastating effect on aggregate benefits,[16] and in very recent times the government has legislated explicitly (granted, under very heavy trade union pressure) to extend the immunities of the 1906 Act to all employees including civil servants.[17]

These developments seem to reflect a growing acceptance within Irish society that one can indeed securely distinguish between the functions of the government in its role as a government and the functions of the government in its role as an employer. Such a view was greatly fostered by the experience of the national pay agreements in the decade of the 1970s. From an early stage, indeed from 1972, the government took its place as an employer on the employer's side of the Employer Labour Conference. In this role however, they were represented at all times by senior civil servants and not by any ministers of government. This was not a haphazard decision but one that was most carefully contrived. The problem was that the trade unions had become extremely sensitive to the role of government in the matter of pay. The general organisational scheme for the joint management of price and incomes had been debated very intensely at the 1970 annual conference of the Irish Congress of Trade Unions[18] and was rejected on the grounds that the involvement of the government in the development of incomes would imply a concession by the trade unions to the social and economic aspirations of the day and this they were not prepared to tolerate. Instead they turned to bargaining with the employers directly, insisting that at all times the organisations created for the purpose should be essentially bipartite in character and never tripartite. When therefore the government representatives took their place with the employers at the table it was clearly understood by all that this in no way disturbed the bipartite character of the negotiations.

On the other hand from time to time it was necessary that the government, qua government, should communicate a view and receive submissions from the parties in relation to economic management but this was achieved by wholly separate conferences conducted in an *ad hoc* manner by government ministers usually with each of the parties separately. In the national understandings

110

of 1979 and 1980, when the government took a much larger hand in creating the context in which the pay bargain was made, this careful isolation of the government's two functions tended as we have seen to break down, but for a substantial part of the period of the seventies it provided a well understood and legitimate distinction, with the consequence that the government's considerable exposure to industrial disputes did not, during that time, invade its strictly political role. On the other hand, of course, it could claim no greater legitimacy for its own actions than any employer in the private sector.[19]

It is against all this background then that we pursue our topic, one in which we consider in a summary fashion the objectives of public authority intervention and then go on to identify the various types of regulation which a public authority may engage in, the legitimacy on which they rest, and the extent to which disputation may follow.

2

Let us reconsider briefly what we have already recognised in regard to public authority objectives and develop on them a little. There are, perhaps, four categories which we can identify, the first to vindicate the rights of a person in relation to his employment, the second to vindicate the rights of a person in relation to the domestic activities of a trade union, the third to regulate relations between employers and trade unions and the fourth to promote social and economic management. We take each of these in turn.

In the case of the first, in the case of the vindication of the rights of a person in relation to his employment, we find an area resting on a broad consensus, much in contrast with interventions the aim of which is the general interest, the public good, that which appears to be politically appropriate, which is a fertile area of dispute. We find such personal vindication in the statutory floor of rights in employment, in the manner for example in which there is provision for adequate conditions of work, in the provision against unfair dismissal and in the provision against discriminating on the grounds of sex. Sometimes, as in the last, it may well be that the public authority, in raising the obligation in a formal way, was somewhat ahead of the consensus, but in general, the identification is one of recognition; it is the formal recognition of a personal right already well-established generally.

But there are personal rights the vindication of which is often challenged, and this we identify as our second category. These are the rights of a person as against the domestic rules of the union, in relation in particular to the closed shop, but also in relation to other jurisdictional matters. The closed shop practices form the heart of the controversy, practices which Conservative thinking found profoundly distasteful. They saw in it perhaps the trade union claim to the *imperium* (which we have already discussed) raising, in the manner in which they conducted their domestic business, problems of a licence to work, of expulsion and of substantial penalties exercised by trade unions in a manner broadly unregulated by the state. It is in these circumstances that the right not to join a union is asserted, and in Mrs Thatcher's Conservative administration it is asserted with increasing vigour irrespective of the circumstances in which the dispute has arisen.

In the third place, there is industrial relations regulation, which in its character has a marked similarity to the regulation of the market. When in the last chapter we discussed a trader's rights in his trade we recognised that the rules upon which the obligations were erected were rules which derived from a widespread commitment to individual competitiveness in trading, not from any intrinsic natural right which the trader possessed. These were market rules which were deemed to be appropriate in the public interest. We see a similar development in industrial relations. There is, first, a desire, in the tradition of individual competitiveness, to establish a balance, an equity, in the influence of the parties.[20] But there is also the question of appropriate conduct, particularly on the part of trade unions, the acceptance of what is regarded as normal market behaviour.[21]

The fourth and final area of intervention is directed to the better economic and political management of the state. Again we can identify a distinction here. There are the general interventions, such as standstills in pay or limits on its development which are the subject of legislative enforcement, and in the second place there are very specific interventions, usually where some industrial action, in the ports for example, or in electrical supply, threaten the safety of the citizens in a considerable way. Here, because of the object of the intervention sanctions on the whole tend to be very fragile.

In this business of enforcement, in the achieving by the public authority of these objectives by regulatory means, we find, in developments in the United Kingdom, two very contrasting strategies, one highly regulatory in character, the other using regulation to support the policy of facilitation. But the first strategy, no less than the second, sought powerfully for a general legitimacy in what it did.

The first strategy is represented in its most comprehensive form by the Industrial Relations Act 1971. It placed industrial relations unequivocally within market place thinking. The odd and unhappy traditions of the common law were replaced by a clear statement of rights and duties, of freedoms and obligations, deriving largely from commonsense market considerations. Associations and unions were strengthened; there was a right to join a union; there was a right in the case of a union to recruit and also a right to bargain, and to be given by the employer such information as was necessary in order to bargain; but in turn bargains should normally be legally enforceable. And all this meant the creation of the National Industrial Relations Court, a branch of the High Court, with exclusive jurisdiction in industrial relations matters. But the notion of a market demanded other principles as well. Above all there had to be the acceptance of the context within which the market operated, that is, the national interest as perceived by a market economy, and here it was required of trade unions that they return responsibility for privilege and that their capacity to act should wholly depend on their continuing to subscribe to such a view of the national interest. In addition notions of trade union membership had to be limited by a traditional individualism which was also a feature of the market, and finally it followed that industrial action being disruptive of the market was absurd. The whole strategy had logic and coherence but to trade

113

unions it was profoundly implausible.

The second strategy was of course that of the Labour government which took office in 1974. It was envisaged in four stages. The first was to return to the original concept of free collective bargaining as it was understood to exist before the enactment of the 1971 Act; the second was to provide quite explicitly for the notion of collective rights, that is legal rights for trade unions and their members, and for the strengthening and expanding of machinery for dispute resolution, this being achieved by Part II of the Employment Protection Act 1975; the third (achieved by Part I of the same act) was to codify and develop the rights of an individual employee in his employment, all explicitly within a legal context; and the fourth was to amend the Companies Acts in order to provide for participation by workers in management. This last led to the Report of the Bullock[22] Commission, which was somewhat of a debacle. The strategy strengthened and legitimated a number of the rights which trade unions claimed they possessed, but it did little to constrain them, trusting instead to their commitment to public order and sensible economic management, a view strongly contested by many elements within the Conservative party.

Let us turn now more precisely to the means of enforcement, developing the discussion under two headings, the judicial institution and the nature of the sanction that flows from it. We discuss the judicial institution first, taking account from time to time of each of the four objectives which we have identified, that is to say, the rights of a person in relation to his employment, the rights of a person as against the domestic rules of the union, industrial relations regulation, and finally political and economic management.

The clearest expression of the vindication of personal rights in employment is contained in the 1975 Employment Protection Act. Apart from extending the jurisdiction of the industrial tribunals the act created a new appellate court for the tribunal system, the Employment Appeal Tribunal largely dealing with questions of law arising not only from dismissal but also from redundancy, equal pay, and sex discrimination. The Tribunal was given the status of a superior court of record, its president being a judge of the High Court or the Court of Appeal; at the same time however there were 'appointed members' drawn from among employers and trade unions, the object being, clearly enough, to enrich the tribunal with actual industrial relations experience, and also to give workers a greater confidence in its use. Indeed the whole endeavour was to create an enforcement procedure which was 'informal, speedy and accessible.' It is remarkable however that the tribunal was confined largely to individual rights in employment; it was not concerned with judgements concerning collective industrial relations. Ireland followed the same broad pattern (although becoming quite odd in making the Labour Court and not the Employment Appeals Tribunal the appellate body in relation to such matters as sex discrimination).

Clearly in this case there was no real difference of view regarding the objective nor indeed regarding the nature of the tribunal. It is perhaps worth noting that in Ireland the idea of a legally qualified chairman was accepted without difficulty when it was most vigorously resisted in the case of the Labour Court. More than that, advocates before the tribunal are often lawyers, a practice which, apart from one unfortunate adventure, is in the Labour Court unknown in industrial relations matters. It probably is the case that such disputes could just as well be disposed of in the ordinary courts of law were it not for problems of delay and expense. When we come to our second category, we find a mixed bag, because we are in fact confronted with two quite different circumstances. As we have already recognised the majority of personal rights cases which arise by reason of the operation of domestic tribunals within trade unions are more properly to be understood as industrial relations disputes (and this was abundantly clear in *Educational Company v. Fitzpatrick*).[23] Nevertheless there are a reasonable number of cases where indeed a personal right is invaded, as in *Meskell v. CIE*.[24] The common law courts in Ireland however made no distinction in principle between the two but we see the distinction clearly enough in the United Kingdom experience, where, when the Employment Protection Act 1975 set out to provide in a special way for the vindication of personal rights, it did

115

not assert any general right not to join a trade union, except in the event of a conflict with religious belief.[25] In regard to our discussion on institutions, therefore, we find no separate provision for the vindication of such rights, and they therefore can be discussed in the general industrial relations context.

The most advanced institution, designed to deal with all industrial relations matters (not merely the last category) and in particular relations between employers and trade unions and offences against the regulations of government was the National Industrial Relations Court, established under the Industrial Relations Act 1971. Its jurisdiction therefore included on the one hand, the prohibition of the pre-entry closed shop, the agency shop, the approved closed shop, bargaining units and sole bargaining agencies, and on the other hand imposed procedures, cooling off periods, strike ballots, and in particular unfair industrial practices, that is the new statutory liability which the act of 1971 had created. While the president of the court was a judge, there was substantial lay involvement in the members of the court, the rules of evidence were greatly relaxed and representation was of the simplest. All this was repealed by the Trade Union and Labour Relations Act, and appeal on justiciable matters was returned to the High Court.

But it was nonetheless an experiment of no little interest. An immense endeavour was made to make the process legitimate if not in the eyes of the trade union leadership at least to the public at large. The extended panoply of requirements and obligations imposed by way of registration, and the recital of those industrial practices that were regarded as unfair although in appearance formidable did not in practice depart from what was seen to be reasonable on both sides. But in particular the flexibility of the new court, the expectation that it would sensitively evaluate the real industrial issues that lay behind a dispute, was seen as the fundamental legitimating instrument. Nevertheless it met with outraged and sustained opposition from the trade unions. The reason for this clearly lay not in the propriety of the obligations which had been recognised but in the very principle of government intervention in this area in the first instance. The Labour party

116

legislation that followed, although perhaps excessively restrained, nevertheless broadly sets out the limits of the general consensus in these matters. There was no difficulty in providing a judicial system for individual rights in employment, and the industrial tribunals were retained, even in relation to workers' rights against a trade union (although much moderated)[26] but in all cases appeal was to the High Court, and while a code of practice was continued it had no statutory effect. A consensus was achieved on the basis of the old system of common law liability, moderated or negatived by certain statutory immunities, which with all its appalling defects in principle was nonetheless seen by trade unions as a more secure basis for their operations.

The Labour Relations Court which has been recommended in the report of the Irish Commission of Inquiry on Industrial Relations[27] was given, as we have already seen, questions for decision which properly were not justiciable at all. Nevertheless it was also given questions which were eminently justiciable, both in regard to breaches of statutory procedures, and also in regard to individual rights in employment which in the United Kingdom are given separate institutional provision under the Employment Protection Act. Once again one sees the concern with speed, accessibility and experience of industrial relations. Each deputy chairman of the court must have a legal background, and such a legally qualified person would preside in cases involving the implementation of statute law (not necessarily in all cases of a justiciable character); and for the rest, the six other members of the court would be drawn, as to two each, from trade unions and employers with two independents. The steady confusion that marks this recommendation probably reduces rather than increases its legitimacy. There is neither security for good judgement nor is there recognition of the chasm, which exists in Ireland no less than in the United Kingdom, between the legitimacy of individual rights procedures and the dispute ridden area of industrial relations.

Let us now turn to sanctions, the teeth of the enforcement as it were. In this quest for legitimacy, in this quest for an area where obligation is clearly accepted, there are two points that we can

117

make. First, there is a considerable area, the area of collective bargains and their breach, were there exists as a rule little more than a moral sanction. In countries other than ours, sanctions for the breach of collective agreements are very much stronger and it was in those circumstances that the Conservative government, under the 1971 Industrial Relations Act, raised a presumption that all such breaches of collective agreements would be actionable except where the parties specifically declared to the contrary. However it became abundantly clear, as we have already seen, that government intervention to such an extent in the collective bargaining area was not seen as legitimate, and employers quite readily, and without the expectation of any return therefrom, joined the trade unions in declarations that such agreements were not the subject of curial enforcement.[28] It is likely enough that much the same sort of response could be expected in Ireland.

In the second place, the nature of the sanction which flows from a judicial institution can strongly influence the legitimacy of the whole exercise. If I set out to convince a person of his intrinsic wrongdoing by the imposition of a penalty, that is one situation; if on the other hand I circumscribe a person's activity by facilitating those injured by him in their endeavour to have restored to them the loss they have suffered, that is quite another. We see this theme recurring quite strongly in the sanctions which are contemplated in this whole field.

Let us construct some elementary categories in regard to the machinery by which sanctions are applied. One may recognise that collectivities engaged in industrial disputes enjoy certain immunities which one may set out to restrict, extending thereby the rights of others as against the collectivities or the individuals that make them up. Here the sanction provides an opportunity to a person who believes himself damaged by industrial action to seek a restoration of what he has lost or an injunction to prevent it. Second, one may require registration, attaching to it such obligations and indeed in particular such capacities as appear appropriate. This complex area is the very centrepiece of much industrial relations regulation, and as far as the construction of sanctions goes, we shall in a moment go on to inquire into it. In

118

regard to the sanction which might arise from it, we shall see that not only may one expose the individuals in a collectivity (or the collectivity itself) to suit in the hands of other citizens, but one may also construct direct penalties. Finally one may by law create certain industrial relations offences to which both these sanctions may attach, the civil and the penal.

Let us take up the rather difficult question of registration. The object here is to regulate the capacity of a trade union to act, in particular to negotiate and to engage in industrial action, to limit, in a word, these freedoms to such organisations as have been recognised formally in some way, that is to say either registered or licensed for the purpose. While employers' organisations theoretically are in the same position as trade unions in this regard, the debate, naturally enough, turns on the question of trade unions and it is in that context that we develop it here.

Registration is a remarkably flexible instrument and not surprisingly has formed an arena within which very conflicting ideas have been promoted, particularly in the United Kingdom. Initially, under the 1871 Act, registration conferred a certain legal personality on trade unions (which in the event proved of questionable advantage) and in doing so gave a certain security to their contracts and trusts. But there was no substantial diminishment of capacity if a union chose not to register. A trade union was a trade union by definition, by reason of its nature and activity, not by reason of its acceptance on a register by a public authority. The 1906 Act, in greatly widening the scope of immunity in regard to industrial action, in no way varied this fundamental position. The Irish government in 1941, building on this earlier legislation, decided to introduce yet another form of registration which they called licensing. This was quite a separate public act, and capacity was very much part of its purpose. Capacity could be affected in two ways. The first concerned the ability to negotiate wages or conditions of work, and here any person or body who engaged in such activity committed an offence unless that person or body was licensed for the purpose or was exempted from the need to hold a licence. Although this at first sight appears to be a very radical and difficult matter, in fact a great deal turns on the manner in which the license is granted. Broadly speaking there are two approaches. One may confer the licence in accordance with predetermined and reasonably modest criteria, related essentially to the size and stability of the union concerned. If the criteria are reasonable, the licensing system is no great burden to the trade union movement and, unofficially at any rate, may be welcomed by them. This was the system enacted by the Irish government under the Industrial Relations Act 1941. But there is an alternative approach. This introduces the notion of performance. If a trade union performs in a manner which, in the view of an independent authority, is contrary to the public interest, then registration may be refused, or if the trade union is a registered one, it may be excluded from the register. More than that, one can require as a condition of registration a number of undertakings which would greatly extend the formal obligations to which a trade union is bound. If the consequence of exclusion from the register is greatly to constrain its capacity so that it can no longer act in a substantive sense as a trade union then the penalty is a severe one.

This latter was the area within which the debate developed in the United Kingdom. In the late 1960s the Donovan Commission raised the question[29] whether certain bodies should be regarded by law as trade unions and certain bodies not, the characteristics of such recognition being determined by statute. It went on to consider the means by which some of the major statutory protections offered in particular by the 1906 Trade Disputes Act might be limited to such recognised or registered bodies, excluding from protection thereby unofficial strikers, for example, on the grounds that a group in such unofficial action, while an association of workers, was not, for the purposes of the proposal, a registered trade union. There was much debate about this in the Commission and, in the event, both a majority and a minority view. The majority (reflecting in general the position of the Conservative party) were strongly of the opinion that trade union immunities should be limited in this way; the minority view, in which George Woodcock[30] shared, opposed such a proposal on the grounds in particular that it would expose unofficial strikers to suit.[31]

When the Labour Government in its white paper of 1969 *In*

120

Place of Strife took up this question, they not surprisingly followed in general the minority view of the Donovan Commission.[32] They proposed that all unions should register, that registration required certain provisions in all union rules, but that if a union failed to register then it (or its executive committee members) should suffer merely a financial penalty. There was no question of removing immunities appropriate to an association of workers because it had not registered itself as a trade union. This was quite clearly an endeavour to promote better trade union practice but with a penalty of a much more limited kind than the removal of fundamental capacity.

When we turn to the early and more explicit Conservative party view, we find considerable emphasis on the significance of registration and the confining, in large measure, of legal immunities to bodies thus registered;[33] and when the Industrial Relations Act of 1971 was later enacted, the idea of registration was much developed, forming indeed the means by which trade unions would be made answerable to the law. An investigatory function was given to the Office of Registrar, a judicial function to the Industrial Court, and a code of practice was promulgated. The ultimate sanction was cancellation of a union's registration, which raised sharply the significance of such a step, that is to say the difference in capacities and immunities between registered and unregistered bodies. While an attempt was made to provide some flexibility in relation to unofficial action, the thrust of the legislation was to develop further the majority view of the Donovan Commission. It caused, as we well know, a storm of protest from the TUC.[34]

Subsequently the Labour Government in 1974, in section 8 of the Trade Union and Labour Relations Act, abolished the Office of Registrar of Trade Unions and Employers Associations and most of its functions, while registration in the form of listing was returned to the Registrar of Friendly Societies. In fact its significance had largely evaporated. 'An unlisted union or association,' remarks Bryn Perrins in a commentary on the provision, 'is however just as much a trade union or employers association as a listed one, if it satisfied TULRA's definition.'[35]

121

What then can we make of all this? In the first place, although we appear to be dealing with the question of capacity there is provided at the same time, an opportunity for legal sanction. It can arise in two ways. It can arise in circumstances where a group of workers, not being a registered trade union, engages in industrial action, that it to say in unofficial strikes and picketing, and it can arise as well where a trade union, properly so called, may be removed from the register or have its licence revoked, confronting it with peril. A very significant aspect of this form of sanction, however, is that it rests not with the public authority, which merely creates the opportunity, but with the employer, or with the person suffering damage, to restrain the activity or to seek restitution for damage done. Although this form of sanction might be regarded as not being a penalty at all, the action of a public authority in exposing a trade union to such a risk is in fact the constructing of what is virtually a penalty. The centre of the debate therefore turns quite correctly on the enabling action of the public authority not on the subsequent action of the person who has suffered damage. In a word we are concerned with penalty.

We can see in the debate in the United Kingdom a very sharp difference indeed between the various parties on the question of the propriety of such intervention. Let us compare the position of the Conservative party not initially with that of the Labour party but rather, for the purposes of direct contrast, with that of the TUC. When the Conservative party were in power and enacted the 1971 legislation, their view apparently was that while well disposed to free collective bargaining they believed that it should be conducted within the framework of the law. They accepted that bodies engaged in such activities quite frequently resort to disruptive activity which is protected by law and which is regarded as permissible in principle. However, because such a power can be very extensive in its destructiveness, the 1971 Act attempted to establish that it could be exercised only by responsible bodies which in their behaviour were subject to some form of public review, and on whom sanctions, if necessary, could be imposed. Implicit in this view, for our purposes, was the exclusion from real trade union activity of any body not accepted for registration or

122

maintained in registration by the public authority. The present Conservative government, and in particular MrTebbit, is much more impatient of disruptive activities even where they are protected by law and the Act of 1982 and his proposals of January 1983 set out to limit the trade union immunities still further. However, for the purposes of our present discussion on registration, we find in the 1971 Act its most advanced expression.

The TUC, for its part, would also strongly maintain the view that collective bargaining should be responsibly engaged in. It would deplore unofficial industrial action, the dominance of unofficial groupings and the fragmentation of trade unions. But the contrast with the Conservative party position lies in this. The TUC would, at the same time, most vigorously oppose the notion of limiting immunities and capacities to registered trade unions where the criteria for registration and the continuance on the register were a matter for the public authority. Again it is not the notion of good order that is challenged here; it is rather a question of the authority from which, in trade union affairs, good order should spring and by which it should be maintained.

We see here very clearly how the objective of public authority intervention greatly influences the legitimacy of the sanction. If it were merely a question of sanction alone, that is to say if the legitimacy of public authority intervention were accepted but merely the extent of it challenged, then one could lighten the sanction considerably and in that way meet any difficulty which workers might raise. And this appears to have been the assumption that the Labour Party actually made in their white paper *In Place of Strife*. Clearly, as government, they had some sympathy with the general thrust of the Conservative position, their criticism probably being that it was somewhat too extreme in practice rather than bad in principle. They attempted to accommodate the trade union position by suggesting a fine rather than deregistration and ran into very heavy weather with the trade union movement on that account. Eventually, in 1974, their Trade Union and Labour Relations Act made nonsense of the whole idea of registration by converting it into a mere listing. This appears merely to be an acceptance of the reality as the Labour Government at the time

123

experienced it. The earlier position, in *In Place of Strife,* probably represents the heart of their position, one which nonetheless was in practice overborne by the very powerful conflict which attended the notion of any government intervention in this area of collective bargaining.

No matter how astutely then we construct these sanctions, no matter how sensitive we are to their *per se* legitimacy, all such endeavour is overwhelmed by the objective of the judicial process which gave rise to the sanction. We have explored the interesting area of registration, which is a special feature of industrial relations, but it is not necessary to explore the rather self-evident field of penalties, beyond perhaps remarking on the extraordinary adventure into vicarious responsibility, the placing of trade union officials in peril for actions of their members for which, in the normal process of English law, they could not be held account-able.[36] There remains then only one general area to be discussed where, whatever the sanction, the whole process is profoundly influenced by the objective of the intervention. This is the area of economic management.

There are two broad topics which we can discern. The first consists of a general intervention such as the imposition of a wage standstill or a wage limitation. These are inevitably resisted in a very public fashion by the trade union movement, although, if the government's judgement is well based, they can find a grudging acceptance. One has here a number of sanctions. One can, on the one hand, exclude from the statutory immunities industrial action designed to breach the government's regulation and on the other hand one can provide for a straightforward penalty in the event of a breach. The latter tends to be the more effective sanction, since in the case of the first the employer himself must be so committed to the government's regulation that he is prepared to take the initiative in exercising the sanction. This frequently is too much to ask and, more than that, it is not unknown, in these matters, for employer and trade union to fall into a conspiracy to circumvent the government intervention in any event.

The second area of intervention is very specific. It arises where a particular dispute appears to the government to threaten the public interest. Two contrasting Irish cases illustrate the point. The first concerns the Electricity Supply Board (Special Provisions) Act 1966, enacted hastily during the course of a strike of maintenance fitters in the Board, but applied for the first time in 1968 during a strike of general workers.[37] The object of the intervention was to forbid, under penalty, the picketing of Electricity Supply Board installations. In the event some workers, picketing a power station in Dublin, were prosecuted, fined and when they refused to pay the fine, were jailed. The uproar was considerable; the fines were discharged by the Electricity Supply Board who also provided taxis to bring the workers home. This was a very dramatic example of the sanction carrying no legitimacy whatever by reason of the nature of the intervention. The loss of legitimacy could perhaps be attributed broadly to two reasons. The first reason of course was its specific character. Rules to be effective should be general in their application, insofar as it is possible to make them so, and the very specific nature of this enactment made it intrinsically questionable. Secondly the intervention by the government was for a reason external to the dispute as each party understood it. The government itself was concerned with the public welfare and the perils that would arise if electricity supply were discontinued. The reason for the dispute, however, turned on pay and the emotions that surrounded it. Yet intervention by the government, although not directed in any way to a judgement on the issue, nevertheless would have had the effect of greatly strengthening the hand of the employer and weakening that of the trade union.

The second illustration is a contrasting one.[38] In 1973 a national pay agreement was in operation, supported both by the employers and the trade unions. However the Irish Associated Banks and the Irish Bank Officials' Association, the employer and the trade union, were not parties to the agreement and in the event, despite considerable anxiety and pressure on the part of the government, set out to establish a higher pay increase than that which operated generally. The government in these circumstances enacted the Regulation of Banks (Remuneration and Conditions of Appointment) (Temporary Provisions) Act 1973 which provided for a penalty specifically on the Associated Banks if they granted an

125

increase greater than that established under the national pay agreement. Although the Irish Bank Officials' Association protested most vehemently, the trade union movement on the whole remained silent and the measure was successful. In this case perhaps the very specificity of the measure was very much moderated by the fact that it was designed to support a general agreement which was already in operation.

There is a final reason for the fragility of the sanctions springing from this form of intervention whether of a general or a specific kind. When governments intervene in such circumstances they may well do so not so much as an uncommitted moderator attempting to strike a reasonable balance, but often as a third party with its own special interest to pursue, and where such an objective becomes dominant the legitimacy of the intervention, and any sanction that results from it, is much diminished.

3

In summary then, those engaged in industrial relations reform clearly perceived that the judicial institution and the sanctions that it applied had to carry broad acceptability; and therefore much was done to recast the law of wrongdoing in an uptodate way, to construct the court itself in a manner which would make it manifestly more sensitive to industrial relations problems, and to base sanctions more on the principle of restitution in regard to damage done to others than on public penalty. But all this was to little avail. There was a problem there of course. The ordinary courts of law were insensitive to certain situations, were slow, expensive and cast by many trade unionists in a hostile role. But this was not the major difficulty by any means. The problem lay instead in the objective which the public authority had in providing for such interventions, for such institutions, in the first place. Where that objective was supported by a broad consensus, as it was in the case of personal rights in employment, little difficulty arose; where it was not, then the elegance and effectiveness of the judicial structure was ultimately neither here nor there.

The objective of economic and social management and the creation of offences by the government so that such an objective can be secured is a further dimension of this. In all probability however, it should be recognised as a separate and less complex phenomenon. I say this because the other objectives, and in particular those which reveal a consensual rift, spring from profoundly conflicting understandings in our society of what is right, while the objective of government, engaged in the business of economic management, is in normative terms a simpler affair, validated almost in an *ad hoc* manner by what the country would regard as reasonable at the time.

CHAPTER FIVE

Consequences

1

We have based this analysis on the notion of obligation. We have understood it in a frankly juridical way where its essential meaning lies in the consciousness of having an obligation, the acceptance of a responsibility, not merely the experience of being obliged. This is given primary place in our understanding, and from it flow notions of rule, notions of law, judicial institutions, and above all the problems associated with their effectiveness, their acceptability.

Dunlop, in his highly influential but strangely inadequate study,[1] provided us at least with the concept of various actors in the arena of industrial relations, a concept which we have used in the elaboration of the idea of obligation. We dwelt first on the freedoms which all men possess in a free society, in order to examine, as all juridical systems must do, the limits of these freedoms, limits determined by the obligations which the actors owe to others. It is these obligations therefore which provide the framework of the system. Where they are strongly felt the system is secure; where they are challenged, where they are denied, there we find industrial conflict. This latter is the area of interest, first for the purpose of seeking out the reason why, and second - which is near to the heart of all reformers — for the purpose of identifying such changes, perhaps in institutions, perhaps in policies, which would lead to a system more orderly and more satisfactory than that which we now possess.

Some difficulties in our industrial system have arisen merely because of confusion, and this is particularly the case in the area of disputes as to interest, where no law, no rule exists which would render the dispute justiciable. It is right of course to recognise the thrust towards justiciability, the thrust that finds expression in the elaboration of procedures, on the one hand, and, on the other, in the

129

relying on some notion of right or of reasonableness in order to construct a rule; but however one might question the appropriateness of such rules the fact still remains that there persists in the decision-making the notion of an anterior principle of right to which one is giving expression, much in contrast with a third view of how the dispute might be settled which rests on no greater judicial base than an expectation that it might be acceptable to the parties.

But where obligation does exist, where it operates so as to limit the freedom to act of the various actors whom we encounter, it does so in the environment of a market. It is probably true, certainly in Ireland, that a very substantial number of those employed are not in a market, or if they are, they are buffered from its effects, yet the idea of the market and the principles of the market still tend to be the ultimate orthodoxy even here. It is an orthodoxy which appears to spring from a belief in the small independent trader and his defence, so that large undertakings, monopolies and cartels are all intrinsically questionable, and for our purposes, this notion of the wrongfulness of combinations of any kind extends inevitably to collectivities of workers. But, as we have seen, while trade unions bitterly contest this denial of their legitimacy, they appear to accept in practice the particular orthodoxy of the market from which their difficulty actually springs. In theory, of course, they do not, but trade unions as we know them today would no longer exist if in fact the socialist dream were achieved, but would become something quite other, as is so clearly the consequence in Eastern Europe. There is an instinctive commonsense therefore in the acceptance of the market orthodoxy, no matter how wrongheaded and illogical it might be to a person of a socialist disposition, and indeed to others as well.

Nevertheless the problems it presents are severe. The intrinsic illegitimacy of trade unions, although much moderated by statute, creates a great normative chasm. The freedom to act, on the part of a collectivity, is always in question; the idea of a collectivity possessing rights is denied. And this is not merely a tradition of the common law; it is intrinsic to the market system, however much it might be moderated in the ordinary business of living. Once one recognises this, one recognises where the area of disputation must lie. There is little or no difficulty in regard to personal, or individual, rights, but where a collectivity, *qua* collectivity, becomes involved, then the normative chasm appears. It invades areas where clear rights actually exist which in the normal course of events should be justiciable. A denial of individual rights by an employer is actionable in the United Kingdom before the Employment Appeal Tribunal; a denial of individual rights by a trade union is not, indicating not its inherent lack of justiciability (because of course it is actionable *per se*) but the difficulty of handling the issue when a collectivity is involved. More than that, rights and obligations arising from collective agreements are regarded (sometimes of course, wrongly) as not being justiciable matters. Granted there are certain legal difficulties involved, but these have been solved by countries other than the United Kingdom and Ireland. Once again it represents the lack of consensus, the lack of a secure base of right upon which the obligations can be erected.

In the eyes of reformers, therefore, it is this normative chasm which must be bridged. But prudence would seem to indicate that one should not contemplate a vast bridging all at once, but rather, because notions of legitimacy vary so much from one employment to another, a painstaking and careful elaboration of the idea of binding obligation specifically in the context of each particular employment, and in accordance with the consensus that exists there.

But are these things possible? Some would say that the political and social system in the United Kingdom and in Ireland makes advances in this area very unlikely. Others, in support of the same opinion, speak of the very culture of our societies inhibiting such a development. What then are the prospects of a substantial reform? Certainly, as far as Ireland is concerned, New Zealand offers an interesting comparison, providing, at first sight, an appearance of a dramatically different system from that which exists here, and on the other hand providing, at the more fundamental level of the legitimacy of institutions, a remarkable similarity in the areas of normative agreement and disagreement.

In their industrial relations systems, Ireland and New Zealand,[2] so similar in their demographic and industrial characteristics, are indeed poles apart. The system in Ireland is usually described as voluntarist, by which is meant that collective bargaining and collective action lie at its centre, and early legislation while failing to domesticate trade unions within the law, provided a licence for collective dispute activity which collectivities other than trade unions did not possess, reinforcing the notion of self-regulation, however inadequately achieved, rather than state regulation. The New Zealand system on the other hand celebrates the rule of law in industrial relations and the role of the state in its administration. There is no 1906 Act to confer special privileges on workers acting in contemplation or furtherance of a trade dispute. Instead trade unions are registered in a manner which greatly regulates what they may do, confers capacity to bargain but only in limited matters and confines their membership recruitment only to specified workers in specified areas. Since the Industrial Conciliation and Arbitration Act of 1894, strikes and lockouts are illegal, except in restricted circumstances, and we find, in place of the free collective bargaining system, one in which there is a two stage judicial process, conciliation and arbitration, the latter leading to a final and binding decision, with an appeal to the Court of Appeal only on a point of law.

These ideas still underlie the formal machinery of the system as is clear from the Industrial Relations Act 1973, and greatly influence the policies and structure of both the trade unions and employer's organisations. And yet in practice the system is changing and in changing reflects the same profound problems of normative disagreement which beset both the Irish and the British systems.

In the first place we are confronted with a fascinating contradiction. Penalties for strike action are severe (picketing is not a prominent feature of the system); substantial damages can be awarded against a union's funds, and there are criminal penalties as well which may be imposed both on trade union officials and striking workers. And yet the incidence of strikes is much greater than in Ireland, in New Zealand very short strikes being common and occurring more frequently than in Ireland, which suffers from a smaller number of more intractable disputes and therefore more mandays are lost. But the point is made.

This raises the question of the effectiveness of the law in inhibiting strike action. There are restricted areas where strike action is not unlawful. These — not surprisingly in the light of our analysis here — occur in disputes as to interest. Since 1973 it is no longer compulsory to refer a case to arbitration if there is a breakdown at conciliation level, and therefore, if a union withdraws the dispute from arbitration, it may proceed legitimately to strike action, or such appears to be the general view. In practice the vast majority of such disputes as to interest are settled at conciliation level. Very few are submitted to the Arbitration Court. Nevertheless, despite limited legality, despite the reluctance to come to final judicial determination, strike action is very much more circumscribed by the law than in Ireland, and yet its magnitude as a phenomenon is not dissimilar.

It appears that since the 1950s the Labour Department, recognising that prosecutions for strike action far from helping now hindered the resolution of disputes, largely discontinued the practice, and when the government experimented once again with the idea in 1976, it had to abandon it for the same reason. Deregistration is always an alternative, and deregistration in New Zealand is a substantial penalty, but this also represents a certain unpinning of the very system which it is intended to defend.

The normative difficulties therefore are similar. The Arbitration Court, in disputes as to interest, is not governed by antecedent law, but rather by some principles such as fair comparison (which tends to create a structure of relativities) and by a concern for the underpaid. But equity is only indifferently achieved in such circumstances since local bargaining can build additional tiers of pay increase, and in any event the principles themselves are uncertain.

On the other hand what does emerge strongly, what does mark New Zealand off from Ireland, is the acceptance by workers of unilateral wage determination by the state. In the 1970s these decisions were made with little consultation, and while tripartism developed during the 1980s because of union pressure, a twelve month wage freeze was imposed in June 1982, and has operated.

It does appear therefore that one can distinguish between two grounds of normative conflict. The first concerns disputes as to interest where no antecedent law exists and the second concerns the intervention by the state, either to impose procedures on the industrial relationship or to determine income levels for the purposes by economic management. It is in the second area that experience differs very much from country to country, a great deal depending on the trade unions' experience of the state and the extent of its dependence on it for equity. There is little doubt for example that in the early years in New Zealand compulsory arbitration was actively sought by the trade unions, because, in their weak condition, they had no other means of ensuring that gains could be achieved.

3

This brings me to a final point, yet another consequence of the analysis which we have attempted here. In a very challenging article in the *International Labour Review* Johannes Schregle, in considering the problem of international comparison in industrial relations,[3] recently urged the wisdom of a *tertium comparationis,* that is 'a third factor to which the industrial relations systems or phenomena of the countries being compared can be related, a third element which provides the yardstick making international comparison possible.' This has since become the subject of international debate.

Dr Schregle was primarily concerned with the identification of standards or values in the administration of industrial relations systems, and he suggested as a *tertium comparationis* the standard-setting activity of the International Labour Organisation. In elaborating the idea he urged the wisdom of looking to the functions which lie behind ideas such as labour courts, collective bargaining and worker participation, but although he pursued the idea bravely the notion of function converted the *tertium comparationis* from a universal standard to a sensitive point of departure in a world of great subtlety and uncertainty. Yet the notion of a *tertium comparationis* remains a very powerful one which perhaps might be given a more concrete and more reliable form by having regard to some of the juridical principles which we have discussed in this study. The distinction between a dispute as to interest and a dispute as to rights is a secure one. The notion that judgement implies some antecedent law is equally secure. And in proceeding in this way we can identify the broad areas where the law is the law of the agreement, where the law is the law of individual rights and where the law is that which the state enacts. To recognise the law is one thing; to evaluate its effectiveness is another, and on this turns the whole system of sanctions which one calls up in its support, because if the law is not based broadly on consensus then its enforcement is uncertain. These ideas, these concepts form, in my view, the true *tertium comparationis* which, while not perhaps wholly universal, are widely shared. Against such ideas we can seek more securely an understanding of the vast majority of institutional forms which industrial relations casts up throughout the world.

1.   Alan Ryan, *The Philosophy of the Social Sciences* (London 1976), p.142.
2.   See Nico Stehr, 'Sociological Language' in *Philosophy of the Social Sciences*, Vol.12, No.1, (Waterloo, Ontario) March 1982.
3.   H.L.A. Hart, *The Concept of Law*, (Oxford 1978) p.86.
4.   Idem.
5.   Idem.
6.   Op. cit., p.87.
7.   Op. cit., p.88.
8.   Auguste Comte, *The Positive Philosophy*, trans. Harriet Martineau (London 1896), reproduced in J.H. Abraham, *Origins and Growth of Sociology*, (Harmondsworth 1973).
9.   Alan Ryan, op. cit. p.216. Some social scientists will of course find a place for notions of justice or fairness in their models as when Glenn A. Withers discussed the Rawlsian theory of justice *(British Journal of Industrial Relations* xv, 3, p.332) but the model remains categorical and logical and never reaches the idea of personally experienced obligation.
10.   Jeff Coulter, 'Remarks on the Conceptualisation of Social Structure' in *Philosophy of the Social Sciences*, op. cit., p.42.
11.   Alan Ryan, op. cit. p.143.
12.   H.L.A. Hart, op. cit. p.88.
13.   Emile Durkheim, *The Division of Labour in Society*, trans. George Simpson (New York 1933), reproduced in J.H. Abraham, op. cit., p.160. For an interesting discussion of ethnomethodology in all this see Jeff Coulter, op. cit. p.33.
14.   John Dunlop, *Industrial Relations Systems*, (New York 1958).
15.   Allan Flanders, *Management and Unions: The Theory and Reform of Industrial Relations*, (London 1975).
16 Allan Flanders, op. cit. p.220.
17.   John Dunlop, op. cit. p.6.
18.   In passing perhaps we might ask ourselves how and in what sense a political system might differ from an economic system in a manner which renders them mutually exclusive, while variations within a system (which arguably should carry some exclusivity about them and consequently should be fissiparous) nevertheless have not this effect. The answer lies of course in the fact that where in a system or a model we introduce variations these are variations of the characteristics that we attribute to a category; they are not variations of the categories themselves or in the logical relationships that exist between them. Indeed such variations in characteristics are a necessary part of system building, the intention being to refine the whole structure and thereby increase its explanatory power.
19.   If one derives obligation exclusively from the notion of the duty one owes to another, one is confronted with the difficulty of regarding attempted suicide, for example, as a punishable offence. Fortunately, it is not an area which needs concern us here.
20.   See for example Mary Redmond, 'Towards a Hohfeldian View of the Rights and Freedoms in the Irish Constitution' in *Dublin University Law Journal*, 1979-80, p.55.
21.   *Crowley and Ors v. Ireland, the Minister for Education, the Attorney General, the INTO and Ors.* 1978 (unreported). See also F.F.V.R. von Prondzynski, 'Constitutional Law — Rights in Balance', in *Dublin University Law Journal*, 1981, p.82.

22.   So much is owed to Kant in all this, who saw in a society which conforms to law, those conditions under which the arbitrariness of one person can be unified with the arbitrariness of another in accordance with a general law of freedom, the maxim being that what he wills can at any time be considered the principle of a general legislation.

23.   John Rawls, *A Theory of Justice,* (Cambridge, Mass. 1972).

NOTES TO CHAPTER TWO

1.   Allan Flanders, op. cit., p.213.

2.   See also Charles McCarthy, 'Worker Participation and the Commission of the European Communities' in *Discussion Papers in Industrial Relations* Vol I, Trinity College, 1981.

3.   An adversary institution working within some consensual context is very well understood and is part of our political tradition. In the Parliament of Westminster the idea is happily summarised in the phrase 'Her Majesty's Loyal Opposition.'

4.   For an early and influential formulation of this view, see Sir William Erle, 'The Law Relating to Trade Unions' in *Tracts on Trade Unions,* (London 1868), also separately published (London 1869); see also the eleventh and final report of the Royal Commission on Trade Unions 1869, Sessional Papers Vol. XXI, 1868-69, (20) p.235. Erle's view was quoted with approval by Budd J. in *Educational Company v. Fitzpatrick* %1961—I.R. 345, at p.367.

5.   See Charles McCarthy, *The Decade of Upheaval,* (Dublin 1973), p.189.

6.   Allan Flanders, op. cit., p.220.

7.   See W.E.J. McCarthy, and N.D. Ellis, *Management by Agreement,* (City 1973), p.41.

8.   Industrial Relations Act, 1946, s.4.

9.   See Michael McGinley, 'Pay Negotiation in the Public Service', *Administration,* (Dublin, Spring 1976), 24, 1, p.76. Mr William Norton, who was largely influential in establishing the civil service conciliation and arbitration scheme was General Secretary of the Post Office Workers' Union from 1924 to 1957 and Tanaiste (Deputy Prime Minister) in 1950.

10.   See Charles McCarthy, *Trade Unions in Ireland* 1894-1960, (Dublin 1977), p.544.

11.   See Charles McCarthy, *Decade of Upheaval,* op. cit. p.58. See also *Annual Reports* (Irish Congress of Trade Unions, Dublin 1962), p.264 and 1963, p.239.

12.   Industrial Relations Act 1946, s.68 (1).

13   *The Labour Court: Twenty-third Annual Report* (for 1979), p.5.

14.   Industrial Relations Act, 1969, s.19.

15.   *Report of the Commission of Inquiry on Industrial Relations,* (Dublin, Stationery Office, 1981) Pl.114, p.100.

16.   See Charles McCarthy and David Dillon: *Freedom and Obligation under the law* (Dublin 1981), Chapter 3.

17.   Trade Union Act 1871, s.4.4.

18.   Idem, s.3.

19.   *Ford Motor Company Ltd., v. A.E.F.* [1969], All E.R. 481.

20.   *Goulding Chemicals Ltd. v. Bolger* [1977], I.R. 211.

21.   Kadar Asmal: *The Law on Collective Agreements in Ireland,* 1977, (unpublished), Submission to the Commission of the European Communities, in the Department of Law, Trinity College Dublin.

22   *Transport Salaried Staff Association v. Coras Iompair Eireann* [1965], I.R. 180.

23.   O. Kahn-Freund, *Labour and the Law* (London 1977) p.138.

24.   Some scholars in Warwick University surveyed the consequences of this provision in the 1971 Act and found employers on the whole indifferent to it, and ready, without bargaining advantage, to include disclaimers. See Brian Weekes, Michael Mellish, Linda Dickens and John Lloyd, *Industrial Relations and the Limits of Law* (... 1975) p.159, where it is stated: 'Securing compliance with agreements did not emerge as a major problem from our interviews with management. On the whole managers were satisfied with their industrial relations and did not want to involve the law. Where companies told us that they had difficulties securing compliance with agreements, they tended to be related to other issues, like the informality of negotiations, or the sectional nature of bargaining. We did not interview any manager who had tried to bargain seriously about putting a disclaimer in agreements, or who thought that the introduction of legal sanctions ensured that "agreements are really meaningful and are carried out by all parties."'

25.   *Report of the Royal Commission on Trade Unions and Employers' Associations,* Cmnd. 3623, (London, HMSO 1968), para 502.

26.   Charles McCarthy, *Trade Unions in Ireland,* op. cit., 1977, Chapter 12

27.   Charles McCarthy, idem.

28.   Charles McCarthy, *The Decade of Upheaval,* op. cit., Chapter 3.

29.   Charles McCarthy, 'A Review of the Objectives of National Pay Agreements', *Administration,* (Dublin) 25, 1, 1977.

30   *The Labour Court: Twenty Third Annual Report* (for the year 1969) Prl. 1308 (Dublin, Stationery Office, 1970).

31.   See Charles McCarthy, 'Productivity Agreements: the Problem of the Spurious' in *Journal of Irish Business and Administrative Research* 4, 1 (Dublin, April 1982), p.99.

32.   A particular difficulty arose on the amalgamation in 1967 (see *Annual Report,* Irish Congress of Trade Unions, 1967) of the Irish Engineering, Industrial and Electrical Trade Union and the National Engineering Union to form the National Engineering and Electrical Trade Union. The electrician members of the first union, finding themselves, by reason of the access of numbers among their engineering colleagues, in a very diminished minority, challenged the amalgamation in the courts, and some subsequently were associated with a breakaway electricians' union.

33.   See *Review Body on Higher Remuneration in the Public Sector:* Report No 20, (Dublin, Stationery Office, 1979), Prl. 8148, in particular chapter I.

34.   See in particular, *The Labour Court - Thirty First Annual Report* (1977), (Dublin, Stationery Office), Prl. 7100.

35.   This raises a complex problem. The Labour Court, in its general policy, tends to recommend in cases coming before it increases which are in conformity with such general movements in pay as exist at the time. It tends therefore to stabilise and confirm, so much so indeed that in disputes where workers are seeking a departure from the general norm they are reluctant to avail of the Labour Court (See for example: Con Murphy, *Report of Inquiry: Dispute between FUE and Maintenance Craft Unions,* (Dublin, Stationery Office, 1969), Prl 798, p.15). This is, however, a matter of commonsense. General movements in pay arise either spontaneously or by national agreement. The Labour Court, in the task of examining disputes one by one, does not normally set out to create any general movement; this is a matter for national bargaining. It follows therefore that it will tend to conform to such movements, whether nationally agreed or spontaneous. But it is a matter of respect for a general wish, not a matter of obligation, as the Court itself makes clear in its *Thirty-third Annual Report* for the year 1979.

36.   *Report of the Commission of Inquiry on Industrial Relations,* (Dublin, Stationery Office), 1981, Pl. 114.

37.   Charles McCarthy, *Trade Unions in Ireland,* op. cit., p.532.

38 Charles McCarthy, *Trade Unions in Ireland*, op. cit.

39. Charles McCarthy, 'Reform: A Strategy for Research' in *Reform of Industrial Relations*, ed. Hugh M. Pollock, (Dublin 1982).

NOTES TO CHAPTER THREE

1. H.L.A. Hart, op. cit. in particular Chapter V.

2. Kenny, J. in *Murtagh Properties v. Cleary* [1972], I.R. 330 at p.335 and confirmed by Walsh, J. in *Murphy v. Stewart* (1973) I.R. 97. See also *Bunreacht na hEireann, Constitution of Ireland:* Preamble.

3. Nagle v. Feilden [1966] 2 Q.B. 633 at p.650.

4. Supreme Court, unreported, 30 April 1981. See Ferdinand von Prondzynski and Charles McCarthy, 'Case and Comment' in *Dublin University Law Journal*, 1981, p.99.

5. In order to appreciate the reason for this, one might consider the remarks of Mr Justice Lavery in *The Educational Company of Ireland v. Fitzpatrick* [1961] I.R. 323. 'The (interlocutory) injunction is merely provisional in its nature and does not conclude a right. The effect and object of the injunction is merely to keep the status quo until the hearing or further order. In interfering by interlocutory injunction the court does not in general profess to anticipate the determination of the right, but merely gives it as its opinion that there is a substantial question to be tried and that until the question is right for trial, a case has been made out for the preservation of the property in the meantime in status quo. A man who comes to the court for an interlocutory injunction is not required to make out a case which would entitle him at all events to relief at the hearing. It is enough if he can show that he has a fair question to raise as to the existence of the right which he alleges and can satisfy the court that the property should be preserved in its present actual condition until such can be disposed of.' But in a labour dispute what is the status quo? How can it be determined? The law here appears to be that the principle of the balance of convenience comes into play. Where a doubt exists as to the plaintiff's right, or if his right is not disputed but its violation is denied, the court, in determining whether an interlocutory injunction should be granted, takes into consideration the balance of convenience. In a word it asks itself the question: 'What would be the extent of the damage suffered by the defendant if the injunction were granted and if in the event he was shown to have acted lawfully?' Against this is balanced the extent of the damage which the plaintiff would suffer if the injunction were not granted. It can readily be seen that in such circumstances a trade union is in some difficulty. Once picketing for example in an industrial dispute is enjoined at the interlocutory stage the dispute from the trade union's point of view is well-nigh lost. The final hearing of the action is too remote to be significant. When in addition the balance of advantage is judged solely in financial terms (as is the case in Ireland although not necessarily in the United Kingdom) then the trade union finds itself on remarkably weak ground. (See also von Prondzynski and McCarthy, 'Case and Comment', in *Dublin University Law Journal*, Trinity College Dublin 1981, p.101.)

6. Sir William Erle, *The Law Relating to Trade Unions* (London 1869), p.51.

7. *Educational Company of Ireland v. Fitzpatrick* [1961] I.R. 323.

8. We discuss later whether and in what sense a trader possesses an actual right in these circumstances.

9. Sir Henry Sumner Maine, *Ancient Law* (London 1878), p.170.

10. Franz Mestitz, 'The Right to Work — the Legal View' in *Universitas*, (Stuttgart 1979), 21, 1, p.2.

11. In the United Kingdom the consensus is not only well-documented but extended to

quite detailed matters. The Donovan Commission (paras 530-567), the white paper *In Place of Strife* (paras 103-4), the Industrial Relations Act 1971 and the Guide (paras 42-53) all reinforce or elaborate on the same principle. The Trade Union and Labour Relations Act of 1974 explicitly re-enacted the provisions regarding dismissals that were contained in the Act of 1971, and while they were modified by the Employment Act 1980 they have remained essentially the same.

12. *Fair Deal at Work* (London 1968), p.42.

13. See Unfair Dismissals Act 1977; see also Redundancy Payments Acts 1967-79, Maternity Protection of Employees Act 1981, Minimum Notice and Terms of Employment Act 1973, Employment Equality Act 1977, Anti- discrimination (Pay) Act 1974.

14. This point we explore later in regard to sit-ins and similar forms of industrial action.

15. It was provided that in the case of a charge that the employer had acted unreasonably the onus of proof was shifted to the employee.

16. See a very full report in the *Irish Times,* 30 August 1976.

17. Charles McCarthy, *The Decade of Upheaval,* op. cit., p.133.

18. Con Murphy, *Dispute between FUE and Maintenance Craft Unions,* (Dublin, Stationery Office 1969), Prl.798.

19. Brian Weeks etc. *Industrial Relations,* op. cit. p.6. See also 'Chronicle' in *British Journal of Industrial Relations,* (London), XII, 2, July 1974.

20. Trade Union Act 1871.

21. *Taff Vale Railway Co. v. Amalgamated Society of Railway Servants* [1901], A.C. 426.

22. International Labour Organisation, *Convention 87: Freedom of Association and Protection of the Right to Organise* (Geneva 1948).

23. *The Observer,* 26 October 1975, p.3.

24. See Irish Congress of Trade Unions, *Annual Report,* 1964, p.91.

25. See 'Chronicle' in *British Journal of Industrial Relations,* XIII, 1, March 1975, p.131.

26. *Educational Company of Ireland v. Fitzpatrick* [1961] I.R. 345.

27. *Nagle v. Feilden* [1966], 2, Q.B. 633 at p.655.

28. *Edwards v. S.O.G.A.T.* [1971] Ch. 365 at p.382-3.

29. See *Murtagh Properties v. Cleary* [1972] I.R. 330 and *Murphy v. Stewart* (1973) I.R. 97. See also *Tierney v. A.S.W.* [1959], I.R. 254.

30. 'Chronicle' in *British Journal of Industrial Relations,* XII, 1, March 1974.

31. *Royal Commission on Trade Unions and Employers' Associations 1965-68,* (London, HMSO,1968) Cmnd. 3623.

32. Byrn Perrins, *The Trade Union and Labour Relations Act 1974* (London 1975) (1973).

33. *Nordenfelt v. Maxim Nordenfelt Guns and Ammunition Co.* [1894], A.C. 535 T.L.R. 636. See also *White v. Riley* [1921] 1 Ch. 1 and *Crofter Hand Woven Harris Tweed v. Veitch* (1942) A.C. 435.

34. See n.29 to this Chapter.

35. Idem.

36. *In Place of Strife,* op. cit.

37. *Fair Deal at Work,* op. cit.

38. Industrial Relations Act 1971, s.5.

39. Trade Union and Labour Relations Act 1974, s.5.

40. The issue in constitutional terms was first raised in *National Union of Railwaymen v. Sullivan* [1947] I.R. 77, although here the object was exclusive representation rather than an obligation to membership.

41. *Educational Company of Ireland v. Fitzpatrick* [1961] I.R. 345.

42. Meskell v. Coras Iompair Eireann [1973] I.R. 121.

43. *The Case of Young, James and Webster; Judgment,* Council of Europe (Strasbourg)13 August 1981.

44. *National Union of Railwaymen v. Sullivan* [1947] I.R. 77.

45. *Cooper v. Millea* [1938], I.R. 367.

46. See Charles McCarthy, *Trade Unions in Ireland 1894 - 1960,* op. cit., in particular Chapter V.

47. Perhaps it does, to some degree, help to demonstrate the trade union position on discipline in membership, Cooper's case being discipline exercised by a union acting within its own powers, and the NUR case being discipline exercised by way of statutory intervention.

48. *Educational Company of Ireland v. Fitzpatrick* [1961], I.R. 345.

49. *Meskell v. Coras Iompair Eireann* [1973], I.R. 121.

50. *Report of the Commission of Inquiry on Industrial Relations,* (Dublin, Stationery Office, 1981)Pl.114, 1981.

51. See Lord Denning, *Enderby Town Football Club Ltd. v. Football Association* [1971], Ch. p.606 and (1971) 1 All E.R. 215, where he says: 'Has the court power to go behind the wording of the rule and consider its validity? ... if the rule was contrary to natural justice, it would be invalid'. He goes on to cite other instances of invalidity.

52. *Faramus v. Film Artistes Association* (1964) A.C. 925, [1964] 1 All E.R. 25.

53. *Kruse v. Johnson* [1898] 2 Q.B. 91.

54. Perrins, op. cit., (175).

55. *Edwards, v. S.O.G.A.T.* (1971), Ch. 354.

56. Para 628.

57. Indeed such was provided for under s.7 of the Conspiracy and Protection of Property Act 1875. It was repealed by s.2(2) of the Trade Disputes Act 1906. The 1875 Act appears to have concerned itself with communication merely; peaceful persuasion was not covered.

58. *Roundabout Ltd. v. Beirne* (1959) I.R. 423 at p.426.

59. Charles McCarthy, *Trade Unions in Ireland 1894-1960,* op. cit. in particular Chapter XII.

60. Some examples are the strikes of teachers in the 1960s and 1970s and in more recent times those of postal workers. Until very recently those workers not being engaged in trade or industry were not workers for the purposes of the 1906 Act and therefore did not enjoy the immunities which that act conferred.

61. Ferdinand von Prondzynski and Charles McCarthy, 'Talbot (Ireland) Ltd. v. Merrigan' in *Dublin University Law Journal,* 1981, p.99.

62. Op. cit.

63. Charles McCarthy, *Decade of Upheaval,* op. cit.

64. This is particularly evident not only in the 1982 Employment Act in the United Kingdom but also in Mr Norman Tebbit's green paper of January 1983.

65. For a discussion on this and on the general question of property rights in employment see Ferdinand von Prondzynski, 'Property Rights in Industrial Relations' in McCarthy and von Prondzynski, *Discussion Papers in Industrial Relations,* Vol I, McCarthy and von Prondzynski, (Dublin 1982).

66. *Laborem Exercens* (London, 1981), in particular section 12.

67. Charles McCarthy, 'Workers Participation in Ireland: Problems and Strategies', in *Administration* (Dublin), Institute of Public Administration, 23, 2, 1975.

68. For a brief summary see Vester and Gardner, *Trade Union Law and Practice,* 1958, pp.134-5.

69.   This point is not recognised by Sir William Erle, and contributes to the difficulty inherent in his well-known dictum: 'Every person has a right under the law as between himself and his fellow subjects to full freedom in disposing of his own labour or his own capital according to his will. It follows that every person is subject to the correlative duty arising therefrom and prohibited from any obstruction to the fullest exercise of this right which can be made compatible with the exercise of similar rights by others' (Erle, op. cit., p.12). But if he is speaking here of a freedom and not a right, the second part of the statement does not necessarily follow.

70.   The third schedule to the 1972 Act provides a guide to the restrictive practices commissioners on what constitutes unfair practices, but again, as with the court's pronouncements on restraint of trade, each practice is qualified by such adverbs as 'unreasonably' 'unjustly' and 'unfairly', and in any event they are very general in character. They therefore do not provide as good an indication for our purposes as the actual prohibitions.

71.   See John Walsh and Charles McCarthy, *World Law of Competition: Ireland* (New York 1979), Chapter 5.

72.   Restrictive Practices Act 1972, s.5, 1 (1)(a).

NOTES TO CHAPTER FOUR

1.   See Charles McCarthy, *Trade Unions in Ireland 1894-1960,* op. cit., p.383.

2.   See for example Dail Debates, 25 June 25, 1946.

3.   The proposal is set out in National Industrial Economic Council: *Report on Incomes and Prices Policy:* Report No 27 (Dublin, Stationery Office, 1970), Prl.1102.

4.   The debate on the proposal and its rejection is reported in Irish Congress of Trade Unions: *Annual Conference 1970 Twelfth Annual Report,* p.137 and p.273. See also Charles McCarthy, *The Decade of Upheaval,* op. cit., p.179.

5.   James F. O'Brien, *A Study of National Wage Agreements in Ireland* (Dublin 1981).

6.   *National Understanding for Economic and Social Development,* 1979 and *Second National Understanding for Economic and Social Development* 1980 (Dublin) Mount Salus Press.

7.   Jean D. Reynaud, *Problems and Prospects of Collective Bargaining in the EEC Member States:* Commission of the European Communities (Brussels 1981).

8.   Conservative Political Centre: *Fair Deal at Work* (1968), p.10. For an interesting evaluation of developments in the United Kingdom from 1912 to 1982 see Lord Wedderburn of Charlton, 'Introduction: A 1912 Overture' in *Labour Law and the Community,* ed. Lord Wedderburn of Charlton and W.T. Murphy, (London 1982).

9.   *Industrial Relations: A Guide to the Industrial Relations Act 1971:* Department of Employment 1971, p.6.

10.   *Royal Commission on Trade Unions and Employees' Associations 1965-68: Report 1968* Cmnd. 3623 para 39. See also Trade Union Act 1871, s.4.

11.   Under the Trade Union Act 1871 s.4 became necessary in regard to internal contracts with members because s.3 made them justiciable. Perhaps the point should be made that the primary object of these exemptions was not so much to remain aloof but rather to avoid the impossible problem of making a refusal to go on strike a breach of

contract. There were the further difficulties associated with the doctrine of vicarious responsibility.

12. *Fair Deal at Work*, op. cit.

13. *In Place of Strife: A Policy for Industrial Relations* (London, HMSO 1969).

14. The guide-lines of the Conservative government of the early eighties is a case in point. So also was the response of the Irish Minister for Finance in April 1983 when certain large insurance companies appeared to breach the government guide-lines, where the government threatened to impose levies or apply price limits unless their view was recognised (*Sunday Tribune*, 8 May 1983).

15. *Trade Unions in Ireland* op. cit. p.543.

16. S.I. No. 188 1980: Civil Service Superannuation Regulations 1980 Art. 5 Amending s.3 of Superannuation Act 1887. The effect of those regulations was made retrospective to 1 June 1973.

17. Trade Disputes (Amendment) Act 1982.

18. Irish Congress of Trade Unions: *Annual Report* 1970, op. cit.22

19. Perhaps there is one further point we might refer to briefly. This concerns a difficulty the government experiences not so much in its own direct employment area but in the areas in which it exercises considerable but indirect influence, such as state companies, local authorities and so forth. Where the government's role is clear and explicit, and in particular were it is represented at the negotiations, then no great problem exists as far as its legitimacy is concerned (although the difficulties of management might be very great) but where its hand is concealed, where a state company, for example, purports to be acting independently, purports to evaluate as it thinks best the government's position and its own, then where an overriding government influence is widely suspected, considerable tension can follow and this was particularly evident among state companies in the latter part of the 1970s.

20. We see it in the legislation of 1871 and 1906 (and more recently in the Employment Protection Act 1975) where the position of the workers was deliberately strengthened presumably on the grounds that they should be permitted to gain a more commanding position. On the other hand, in more recent times we have seen an attempt to strengthen the position of the employers, in the proposals in the Irish Report of the Commission on Industrial Relations regarding the limits of legitimate industrial action and in Mr Tebbit's 1982 Employment Act which greatly constrains the scope of trade union immunities. These are indeed analogous to the general rules of the market, both in the anxiety about market dominance and also in the anxiety about the general interest which could be affected in a variety of ways.

21. The 1971 Industrial Relations Act in the United Kingdom, as we have seen, introduced the notion of specific offences in a very substantial way by establishing a system of unfair industrial practices, the breach of which could result in an industrial tribunal excluding the union from registration. The Trade Union and Labour Relations Act of 1974 swept all this away but nonetheless, there is much Conservative devotion to the idea, and we see echoes of it once again in the Employment Act of 1980 under which the government issued a statutory code of practice on picketing, the provisions of which are admissible in evidence in proceedings before a court, industrial tribunal or the CAC, and which 'shall be taken into account in determining that question'. The 1972 Employment Act and the proposals of Mr Tebbit of January 1983 set out to restrict further the immunities which the law confers on trade unions, increasing therefore the scope of sanction, while the 1982 Act, as well, in repealing section 14 of the Trade Union and Labour Relations Act, permits a trade union to be sued in its own name for injunction and damages and its funds made amenable for that purpose, where it is established that it has engaged in unlawful industrial action.

143

22. *Report of the Committee of Inquiry on Industrial Democracy* (London, HMSO 1977), Cmnd 6706.

23. *Educational Company of Ireland v. Fitzpatrick* [1961] I.R. 345.

24. *Meskell v. CIE* [1973] I.R.

25. See also Trade Union and Labour Relations Act 1974 Sch.I as amended by Trade Union and Labour Relations (Amendment) Act 1976.

26. Trade Union and Labour Relations Act 1974, 5. See also Employment Protection Act 1975.

27. Op. cit., Chapter 12.

28. Weekes, op. cit.

29 *Donovan Commission,* op. cit., paras 751-800; also reservations pp.380, 289.

30. A one-time general secretary of the TUC.

31. *Donovan Commission,* op. cit., para 804.

32. *In Place of Strife,* op. cit., para 109.

33. *Fair Deal at Work,* op. cit., p.19, and for some exceptions to the general exclusion, p.24.

34. In March 1971 a general conference of the TUC adopted a resolution to the effect that all unions affiliated to the TUC should be advised not to register, a policy which was pursued with some vigour.

35. Bryn Perrins, op. cit., (95). Under the 1975 Act the function passed to the Certification Officer, to whom also was given the function of issuing certificates of independence.

36. See supra.

37. *The Decade of Upheaval,* op. cit., Chapter Four.

38. Idem, Chapter Six.

NOTES TO CHAPTER FIVE

1. John Dunlop, *Industrial Relations Systems,* (New York 1958).

2. In this part of the discussion I have relied heavily on Peter Brosnan and Pat Walsh, *The New Zealand Industrial Reations System: A Case of Too Much Law?* (as yet unpublished).

3. Johannes Schregle, 'Comparative industrial relations: pitfalls and potential' in *International Labour Review,* 120, 1, (Geneva 1981).